For the Love of
PUGS

For the Love of
PUGS

Robert Hutchinson

BrownTrout Publishers
San Francisco

Pugs Photography Credits

Cover		©1998
p.2/3		©1998 Mark Raycroft
4/5		©1998 Jerry Shulman
6		©1998 Jerry Shulman
7	(top)	©1998 Kent & Donna Dannen
7	(bottom)	©1998 Kent & Donna Dannen
8/9		©1998 Jean Wentworth
10/11		©1998 Kent & Donna Dannen
12		©1998 Mark Raycroft
13		©1998 Jerry Shulman
14		©1998 Mark Raycroft
16/17		©1998 Mark Raycroft
18		©1998 Mark Raycroft
20		©1998 Kent & Donna Dannen
22		©1998 Kent & Donna Dannen
23	(top)	©1998 Kent & Donna Dannen
23	(bottom)	©1998 Zandria Muench Beraldo
24		©1998 Sharon Eide
26		©1998 Kent & Donna Dannen
27		©1998 Kent & Donna Dannen
28/29		©1998 Kent & Donna Dannen
30		©1998 Zandria Muench Beraldo
32		©1998 Elizabeth Flynn
33		©1998 Jerry Shulman
34		©1998 Kent & Donna Dannen
36		©1998 W. Holzworth
38		©1998 Mark Raycroft
40		©1998 Mark Raycroft
42/43		©1998 Mark Raycroft
44		©1998 Mark Raycroft
46		©1998 Zandria Muench Beraldo
48		©1998 Mark Raycroft
50		©1998 Kent & Donna Dannen
51		©1998 Mark Raycroft
52		©1998 Zandria Muench Beraldo
54		©1998 Kent & Donna Dannen
56		©1998 Mark Raycroft
57		©1998 Zandria Muench Beraldo
58/59		©1998 Zandria Muench Beraldo
60		©1998 Mark Raycroft
62		©1998 Mark Raycroft
64		©1998 Londie G. Padelsky
65		©1998 Jerry Shulman
66		©1998 Mark Raycroft
68		©1998 Zandria Muench Beraldo
70		©1998 Mark Raycroft
71		©1998 Kent & Donna Dannen
72		©1998 Zandria Muench Beraldo
74/75		©1998 Mark Raycroft
76		©1998 Kent & Donna Dannen
78		©1998 Zandria Muench Beraldo
80		©1998 Londie G. Padelsky
81		©1998 Kent & Donna Dannen
82		©1998 Mark Raycroft
83	(top)	©1998 Kent & Donna Dannen
83	(bottom)	©1998 Zandria Muench Beraldo
84		©1998 Kent & Donna Dannen
86		©1998 Mark Raycroft
87		©1998 Jon Choppelus
88		©1998 Kent & Donna Dannen
90		©1998 Mark Raycroft
91		©1998 Mark Raycroft
92		©1998 Kent & Donna Dannen
94/95		©1998 Mark Raycroft
96		©1998 Jerry Shulman
98		©1998 Kent & Donna Dannen
99	(top)	©1998 Zandria Muench Beraldo
99	(bottom)	©1998 Kent & Donna Dannen
100		©1998 Zandria Muench Beraldo
102		©1998 Sharon Eide & Elizabeth Flynn
103		©1998 Kent & Donna Dannen
104		©1998 Zandria Muench Beraldo
106		©1998 Kent & Donna Dannen
107	(top)	©1998 Jerry Shulman
107	(bottom)	©1998 Mark Raycroft
108		©1998 Kent & Donna Dannen
111		©1998 Kent & Donna Dannen
112		©1998 Zandria Muench Beraldo

Entire Contents
©1998 BrownTrout Publishers, Inc.
Photography ©1998 The respective photographers

Library of Congress Cataloging-in-Publication Data
Pugs / Robert Hutchinson
      p.   cm. — (For the love of—)
    ISBN 1-56313-905-7 (alk. paper)
    1. Pug. 2. Pug—Pictorial Works I. Title. II. Series:
Hutchinson, Robert, 1951–   For the love of—
SF429.P9H88   1998
636.76—dc21
                      98-39143
                        CIP

Printed and bound in Italy by Milanostampa

ISBN: 1-56313-905-7 (alk. paper)
10 9 8 7 6 5 4 3 2 1
Digit on the right indicates the number of this printing

Published by:
BrownTrout Publishers, Inc.
Post Office Box 280070
San Francisco, California 94128-0070 U.S.A.

Toll Free: 800 777 7812
Website: browntrout.com

Little Big Dog

"You humans — when ya gonna learn that size doesn't matter. Just 'cuz something's important doesn't mean it isn't very, very small."

— Frank the Intergalactic Pug,
Men in Black (1997)

So, what did Queen Victoria and Andy Warhol have in common? Well, true enough… they did both have a thing for artwork on red tin cans. But something else.

Stumped? Jeepers, creepers — the answer's staring right at you! Great googly saucer eyes, whose dark lustre flashes with merry to-and-fro between roguish intelligence and eager solicitude. Still guessing?

Okay. Above those big globular eyes, a pregnant little brow puckered into deep-graven wrinkles crisscrossing like a boldly inked Chinese ideogram. Below those glistening eyes, an adorably mushed-in, eminently kissable little mug. Either side of those wide-set eyes, little mobile flaps of black velvet set piquantly high and forward on the skull.

"Come on — stop teasing!" plead the eyes and ears and brow together.

All at once, a chunky jumping-bean burrito is jitterbugging on your lap and excitedly barking the answer to your riddle amidst a flurry of impetuous kisses: "You big dummy — Queen Victoria and Andy Warhol were both just crazy *For the Love of Pugs!*"

Of course, Puggles is far from being just a one-note bundle of jiggling joy. For he is the dog with a thousand faces. The Pug is so versatile an actor that he can slip from role to role with consummate ease. He can begin by insinuating himself into your living room with the polite inscrutability of Peter Lorre scoping a teahouse in Shanghai. Then he can address his emotional attentions to you with the steamroller naïveté of Mickey Rooney on a first date. Finally, he can wind up his routine with all the show-stopper moxie of Jimmy Cagney tap-dancing out in front of a patriotic revue.

Although we cannot fail to be astonished at how skillfully the Pug entertains human beings, we need not be mystified that he possesses this skill. After all, the Pug was

continuously refined for hundreds of years behind the walls of the Imperial City for the sole purpose of diverting the Emperor of China and his retinue of palace courtiers. And the only way a mere dog might hope to amuse this daunting audience — the most sophisticated, subtle, and self-referential microsociety in human history — was if that dog were somehow to remake himself in the image of a human courtier. The Pug succeeded. He polished himself into a funhouse mirror, ludicrously reflecting in a small and cockeyed image the whole precious repertoire of the courtier.

By the time the Imperial Court of China finally collapsed a century ago, the Pug had long since effected its diaspora to safer courts abroad — first the royal courts of Europe; then the numberless domestic courts of the world's new urban bourgeoisie. The Pugs left behind in Peking are an extinguished line, for the Communist Party condemned pet dogs as a bourgeois luxury.

Yet, to this day, the Pug-in-exile retains as his immemorial inheritance all the sleights and savvy of the seasoned courtier. The Pug's instinct still cues him when to retire discreetly behind the wings and when to barrel boldly onto stage. And when he does come on, the Pug still seizes the floor with the fearless forwardness of a guild-jester. He is innately endowed with all the clumsy graces of the court dwarf, who now scowls with jealousy of the imperial dignity of his tiny person; now capers about his master's throne in a breathless fandango. His temper remains imperturbable — even when his heroic struttings and madcap feats of agility are greeted by gales of human hilarity. Neither have his table manners shed the gilded charm of some former age — even when he gives himelf over to riots of gourmandise. The Pug's ardor for comic glory is forgotten only when he is caught up by the silken toils of helpless love. Then is all his ardor but to please his mistress and to take the pleasures of his mistress' lap.

The Pug's very name in French and Italian — Carlin and Carlino, respectively — pays tribute to the breed's comic genius. For Carlino was the stage name of Carlo Bertinazzi (1710–83), the greatest interpreter of Harlequin in eighteenth-century commedia dell'arte. The Pug's resemblance to Harlequin is both temperamental and physical.

Temperamentally, both are faithful, eager, clever, affectionate, good-natured, hedonistic, and irrepressibly high-spirited. Physically, both sport a black half-mask with quizzically arched eyebrows surmounted by an earnestly wrinkled forehead.

Pug's association with commedia dell'arte did not stop with Carlino. One of Harlequin's fellow *zanni* (madcap servants) — Pulcinella — went on to a brilliant career in England. First, beginning in the 1790s, the immigrant Punchinello became the star of the traveling Punch-and-Judy handpuppet shows. Then, beginning in 1841, he took his place as the avatar of that quintessentially English satirical magazine, *Punch*. The magazine's cartoonists would contrive to insert Punch somewhere on the cover of each issue, generally accompanied by his puppet-show sidekick — Toby the Dog. And Toby they drew as — what else? — a Pug.

Down to the present, the Pug's nose for showbiz has lost none of its keenness. Over the centuries, entertainers and artists have gravitated to the kindred thespian spirit of the Pug. Hogarth, Voltaire, Harriet

Beecher Stowe, Sir Ralph Richardson, Rex Harrison, Lena Horne, Sammy Davis Jr., and Andy Warhol all doted on their Pugs at home. On screen, as well, human and Pug actors click beautifully: take Richard Burton and Delila in *Walk with Destiny* (1974); or Tommy Lee Jones and Frank in *Men in Black* (1997). Nor do Pugs require human support to emote effectively — Otis the Pug does a superb job opposite Milo the cat in *Otis and Milo* (1989).

The courts of Europe offered an ideal theatrical setting for the pint-sized Pug's king-sized dramatic talents. The Marquise de Pompadour; Marie-Antoinette; King George III and Queen Charlotte; Empress Joséphine; Queen Victoria; the Duke and Duchess of Windsor; Prince Rainier and Princess Grace of Monaco: all lavished royal largesse upon their Pug favorites.

To be sure — the Pug neither tracks, nor retrieves, nor attacks. He cannot even be counted on to obey with mindless consistency such insultingly simple commands as "Sit!" and "Come!" The Pug can always be counted on, however, to pitch himself with

fine gusto into every witty exchange and every giddy parlor game. Transported to us across gulfs of time and space, how perfectly fitted has this erstwhile cloistered ornament of the Chinese imperial court proven himself to grace the high-rise salons of modern urban sophisticates desirous of a low-activity, low-maintenance, high-living, high-entertainment-value, long-lived little indoor companion!

The Pug personality in all its protean richness is what has captured the hearts of millions of human admirers over the centuries. Personality is a diffusive principle of vital organization; it is not a hard-edged object or event. The action of personality we all feel with warm intensity; yet the cold words at our disposal to describe the springs of the effect are few and fumbling. For the sake of clarity, we therefore forego further discussion of Pug personality. In what follows, we restrict the terms of our description of the Pug to object and event — counting on every Pug lover to put the flesh of personal experience on the bare bones that we lay out.

We will build our picture of the Pug in three mutually intersecting dimensions: physical, genetic, and historical. Starting with the physical dimension, we will look at the crazy little body that houses the giant personality of the Pug. (The Kennel Club Breed Standard for the Pug encapsulates this notion of condensed plenitude in the breed motto: *multum in parvo* — that is, "much in little."). After an appreciative look at the overall body-form and its various points, we will focus upon the Pug's very short-faced head and compare it in shape to the heads of other breeds. We will suggest that the Pug may have had a seminal influence in the genesis of our familiar Western short-faced dog breeds, such as the English Bulldog.

Moving on to the genetic dimension, we will trace the roots of the Pug's head-shape and body-form in the phenomenon of dwarfism and compare the Pug to other dwarf breeds. We will show that the conformation of the purebred Pug depends on the simultaneous operation of four separate dwarfing mutations in its genotype. This chapter is for hard-core Pug nuts. If you begin to bog down in the technical intricacies of this chapter, just skip it and jump ahead to the historical dimension — where any Pug-lover will find nuggets galore.

In the historical sections, we will first recount what is known of the origin and development of the Pug in China. We will advance a new interpretation of the socioethnic significance of the Pug in the culture of the Imperial City, based in part on our preceding discussion of head-shape.

Finally, we will examine what is known about the first appearance of the Pug in Europe. In particular, we will go to some pains to dispute the received wisdom amongst Anglophone Pug-writers that the European Pug has been documented to date all the way back to sixteenth-century Holland. Because its later history receives abundant coverage in the standard Pug literature, we will confine our attention to the first few decades of the European Pug.

Mug Shot

"Life is too short to die with a long face."
— Albert Camus, *The Plague* (1948)

The Pug is a short, solid, square dog. Shortness of back and leg impart to the Pug its basic one-foot-square outline: its one-foot height (ground to withers) equals its one-foot length (point of shoulder to point of buttock). The predominance of perpendicular angles reinforces the impression of the Pug's essential squareness: the topline is level; the legs are straight; and — most distinctively — the head is cubic. In profile, the Pug's startlingly flat face constitutes one face of the cranial cube. Frontally, the Pug's massive head again approximates a square because its skull runs flat between the ears and its slightly undershot jaw extends as wide as the face.

The Pug's high-set tail curls forward and then twists back tightly over one hip or the other. Victorian breeders coyly sought to standardize a rightward curl in dogs and leftward in bitches. A double curl is to die for. Such caudal rhapsodies were lost upon traditional Chinese breeders, who routinely docked their Pugs' tails (and sometimes their noses, too!) in order to cultivate the stubby look of the mythical Chinese spirit-lion.

The Pug's skin is loose and folds into fleshy wrinkles on the face, throat, and neck. The Pug's coat is short and double-density: a short glossy overcoat overlies a thick soft undercoat. The ground-color of the coat may be silver-fawn, apricot-fawn, or jet black. (The traditional Chinese Pug admitted all colors and markings.) Markings in the fawn varieties must be intensely black and well-defined: the "mask" on the muzzle; the ears; the cheek moles; and the (optional) "diamond" on the forehead.

By reference to size and function, the American Kennel Club categorizes the Pug with the Toy Dogs. On morphological grounds, however, cynologists assign the Pug to the Mastiff Family (*Molossoides*), where it stands cheek to hock with such giants as the Saint Bernard. Within the Mastiff Family, its extreme shortness of muzzle allies the Pug most closely with the modern Bulldog. Indeed, we shall argue below that the English Bulldog did not acquire its extreme shortness of face and limb until the nineteenth century —

thanks to Pug-crossing. And whom should the English (and hence the French) Bulldog thank for the Pug? China!

How much the pugnacious West owes sedate old China! What schoolchild cannot lisp that resounding list of key Chinese inventions — paper, gunpowder, movable type, magnetic compass, paper money — without which Western civilization could never have emerged from its Middle Ages to engirdle the modern world? A second group of imported Chinese technologies — though clearly less epochal than these great utilitarian inventions — quite as thoroughly transformed the luxury end of Western material culture. Such were silk, tea, porcelain, and brachycephalic dogs.

Brachy-say what? Blame the Greeks. *Brackhus*, "short;" *kephalé*, "head": *brachycephalic*, "short-headed." Strictly, a skull is *brachycephalic* if the ratio of its greatest width to greatest length (from front to back) is large relative to the mean ratio for the whole species population. This width-to-length ratio is termed the *cranial index*. For a given mammalian species, the cranial index of a skull determines its assignment to one of three conventional categories: *brachycephalic*, *dolichocephalic*, or *mesocephalic*.

Consider our own species. A human skull is classified as *brachycephalic* if its width is more than 80% of its length; *dolichocephalic* ("long-headed") if its cranial index is less than 75%; and *mesocephalic* ("middle-headed") if its cranial index falls between 75 and 80%. Before the horrors of National Socialism, schoolchildren were taught that Asians were brachycephalic; Africans dolichocephalic; and Europeans mesocephalic. Such gross paradigms have been thoroughly discredited. The ranges of cranial parameters of any two natural geographic sub-populations of the same species always overlap to some extent.

Nevertheless, each mammalian species is characterized by a peculiar spectrum of skull morphology that determines a characteristic value for the mean cranial index of that species. Dog skulls, for example, tend to be proportionately longer than human skulls, so that the mean cranial index of *Canis familiaris* (58% — if we take the Golden Retriever as the mean breed) is much smaller than that of *Homo sapiens* (78%). Furthermore, the total range of cranial indices in dogs (from 56% for the dolichocephalic Saluki to 108% for the brachycephalic Pug) is wider than that in human beings, so that the numerical interval corresponding to each of the three cranial-index categories is wider for the dog than for man.

Natural populational terms are notoriously tricky. There is an idealizing tendency in primitive human thought that rejoices at such assertions of simple congruence between geography and biology as the unqualified statement that "Asians are brachycephalic." The more sophisticated or conscientious observer ferrets out the inexactitudes of such generalizations about natural populations and spoils the party for the idealist.

Well-managed artificial populations, on the other hand, can gratify in reality the desire for an uncomplicated congruence between name and biological attributes. By artificial selection, human beings can realize in dog breeds those ideals of biological purity that they must fail to impose on their own species. Modern dog breeds are well-managed artificial populations *par excellence*. Go to a Pug show and examine a hundred Pugs: in every case, the congruence between the name "Pug" and any standard Pug attribute such as head shape will be all but perfect.

Because human breeders artificially constrain the dimensional ratios of skulls within a given dog breed to conform to an explicit breed standard, each dog breed fits neatly into one and only one of the three cranial-index categories. Thus, all greyhounds are dolichocephalic; all Chows mesocephalic; all Pugs brachycephalic. In order of increasing cranial index (that is, increasing short-headedness), our common brachycephalic breeds include the Boxer, English Bulldog, French Bulldog, Brussels Griffon, Boston Terrier, Cavalier King Charles. Japanese Spaniel, Shih Tzu, Pekingese, and Pug.

The statistical craniometry of a natural population such as *Homo sapiens* contrasts strongly with that of an aggregate of artificial populations such as our modern *Canis familiaris* pure breeds. The cranial indices for the global human population plots along a smooth bell-curve of normal distribution. The case is quite different for pure breed dogs. As expected from the above discussion, the cranial indices for the global population of dog breeds plots stepwise by breed.

What is less expected is that the dog breed cranial indices plot in a strongly bimodal distribution, as demonstrated by Konrad Wagner in *Rezente hunderassen* (1929). Average cranial indices per breed for the dolichocephalic and mesocephalic breeds are

clustered together in roughly normal distribution between 56% (Saluki) and 68% (Saint Bernard). Average cranial indices per breed for the brachycephalic breeds form a discrete set of values falling in the range of 100 to 113% (based on the database kindly supplied by Dr. Marc Nussbaumer, curator of the dog skull collection of the Albert Heim Foundation for Canine Research, Natural History Museum of Berne). The brachycephalic set of values is totally disjoined from the lower set of non-brachycephalic values.

The lower cluster of dog breed cranial indices corresponds quite closely to the global range of cranial indices per subspecies of the wolf. The cluster of brachycephalic dog breeds, on the other hand, is perfectly remote from the range of natural canid cranial indices. This latter incongruence supports the archeological evidence reviewed by Stanley Olsen in *Origins of the Domestic Dog* (1985) against the notion that the Eastern Asiatic brachycephalic breeds could have evolved from the relatively short-muzzled — but still mesocephalic —

Pleistocene ancestor (*Canis lupus variabilis*) of the modern Chinese wolf (*Canis lupus chanco*).

We contend that the cranial indices of the brachycephalic dog breeds form a class so conspicuously remote from the rest of the canid family because these breeds carry a specific genetic mutation that can be fixed only by artificial selection for precisely the effects of that mutation. The physical effects of that mutation would otherwise render the carrier incapable of surviving to reproductive age either in nature or in human society as a working animal. (In 1997, indeed, the German state of Hesse enacted a law prohibiting the breeding of brachycephalic dogs — including the Pug, Pekingese, and Bulldog — on the ground that they have departed injuriously far from nature.)

Of the brachycephalic breeds named above, only the Pug and Pekingese are patently Chinese in origin. Yet a *prima facie* case can be made that the brachycephaly of all modern Western brachycephalic molossoid breeds (including the English Bulldog, French Bulldog, Brussels Griffon, Boston Terrier, Boxer, Dogue de Bordeaux, Bullmastiff) is ultimately derived from historical Pug-crossing. The essential piece of negative evidence is that true brachycephaly cannot be shown to have occurred in European dogs prior to the importation of Chinese Pugs at the turn of the eighteenth century.

Let us look at the English Bulldog as an example. In *The Animal Estate* (1987), Harriet Ritvo has shown that our modern brachycephalic English Bulldog is the deliberate product of a program of radical redesign in the second half of the nineteenth century aimed at rehabilitating the old-style English bulldog which had declined into total eclipse in the decades following the passage of the Parliamentary bill banning bull-baiting in 1835. The old-style bulldog had in fact not constituted a breed at all, but consisted rather of a motley assortment of individuals widely varying in shape and size who had alike demonstrated the evasive agility, jaw strength, and mental tenacity needed to clamp onto the nose of a maddened bull and cling there indefinitely.

Prior to the second half of the nineteenth century, no graphic representation of any bulldog — whether English bulldog or Continental *Bullenbeißer* — prefigures either the brachycephaly or stunted limbs of the modern English

Bulldog who rose like a phoenix from the ashes of the old-style bulldog in the decade following the founding of the Bulldog Club in 1874. The shortest-muzzled specimens to be found in pictures of the old-style bulldog would qualify — in the quantitative scheme defined above — only as high-end mesocephalic.

The breed that would become known as the French Bulldog originated in the 1860s in the English Midlands as unwanted by-products of an experimental bulldog breeding program that were rejected by their English breeders for dwarfism but welcomed by the French dog fancy for the same reason. The French Bulldog bears a strong resemblance to the European Pug as it appeared before the fresh infusion of Chinese Pug stock in England in the 1870s.

Here lies a likely-looking key to the origin of the innovative features of the modern English Bulldog. We suggest that the breeding program that accidentally created the French Bulldog was engaged in crossbreeding smaller representatives of the old-style bulldog with the European Pug. The hybrids that

retained the Pug's pituitary dwarfism were drowned or shipped to France; those that inherited only the Pug's achondroplastic dwarfism were developed into the modern English Bulldog. The symptomology and genetics of these two types of dwarfism are the subject of the next chapter.

The other Western brachycephalic molossoids can likewise be linked directly or indirectly to Pug ancestry. The crossbreeding program in Munich that resulted in the Boxer at the end of the 1890s, for instance, is reported to have received a contribution from the English Bulldog. This then is the sense in which Western brachycephalic molossoid dog breeds can be said — *pace* the patriotic dignity of the English Bulldog, the French Bulldog, and the German Boxer — to embody a gift from China.

Even Dwarves Start Small

*"Some of the peculiarities of the several breeds of
the dog… may be called monstrosities; for instance,…
the shape of the head and the under-hanging jaw in the
bull- and pug-dog."*

— Charles Darwin,
The Variation of Animals and Plants (1868)

Nowhere did Charles Darwin more explicitly develop his revolutionary idea that species evolve by an incessant interplay between variation and selection than with reference to the origin of dog breeds. In the first volume of his monumental *The Variation of Animals and Plants under Domestication* (1868), Darwin recognized in dog breeds two general classes of inherited traits, distinguished by their contrasting modes of variation and selection. Traits of the first type are those that have arisen through "the selection, both methodical and unconscious, of slight individual differences, — the latter kind of selection resulting from the the occasional preservation, during hundreds of generations, of those individual dogs which were the most useful to man for certain purposes and under certain conditions of life."

In contrast to this first — what might now be termed *adaptive* — class of traits fixed by insensibly incremental selection of slight differences (nowadays called *allelomorphic variants*) according to largely unconscious criteria of usefulness for specific work, inherited traits of Darwin's second class are those that have arisen through the deliberate preservation of radical mutations that confer no working advantage to the dog. "A peculiarity suddenly arising, and therefore in one sense deserving to be called a monstrosity, may, however, be increased and fixed by man's selection." As two instances of this second class of inherited traits in dog breeds, Darwin cites "the shape of the legs and body in the turnspit of Europe and India; the shape of the head and the under-hanging jaw in the bull- and pug-dog, so alike in this one respect and so unlike in all others."

"Turnspit legs" and "pug-dog head": These two examples of Darwin's second, *non-adaptive* class of inherited traits in dog breeds are both manifestations of a genetic disorder called *achondroplasia*. Any genetic disorder in a dog breed that causes certain bones to grow to a length that is

disproportionately short in relation to the rest of the skeleton falls under the rubric of *achondroplasia*. Achondroplasia (literally, "without cartilage formation") acts by inhibiting cartilage formation at certain of the discrete *epiphyseal growth plate sites* distributed throughout the skeleton. Depending on which particular epiphyseal growth plate sites are affected, various achondroplasias are seen to affect specific bones in the different achondroplastic dog breeds. "Turnspit legs" exemplify what is now termed *micromelic achondroplasia*; "pug-dog head" exemplifies *brachycephalic achondroplasia*.

Micromelic achondroplasia targets only the epiphyseal growth plate sites at the proximal ends of the long bones and thus acts to shorten only the dog's limbs, without appreciably affecting its axial skeleton (head, trunk, and tail). The Dachshund and Basset-hound breeds — modern successors of the extinct Turnspit — exemplify the variety of achondroplasia that causes *micromelia* ("small limbs"). On account of their abnormally short stature, the micromelic breeds rank as *dwarves* in the general

zoological sense. But since their axial skeletons generally retain normal size and proportion, the micromelic dog breeds are more narrowly classified zoologically as *achondroplastic* (or *disproportionate*) *dwarves*. (In the nomenclature of the dog fancy, it should be noted, the term *dwarf* is reserved exclusively for *proportionate* dwarves.)

Opposed to the disproportionate effects of achondroplastic dwarfism are the proportionate effects of *pituitary dwarfism* — as seen in dozens of toy breeds such as the Chihuahua, the Pomeranian, the Italian Greyhound, and the Miniature Pinscher. The small stature of the pituitary (or *ateliotic*) dwarf (non-technically, *midget*) results not from any site-specific achondroplastic disorder but rather from a systemic endocrine disturbance (deficient secretion of the hormone *somatrophin* by the anterior lobe of the pituitary gland) that acts to stunt all somatic cell growth proportionally. The stunted features often assume an infantile or neotenic character. Ateliosis is a genetic disorder transmitted as a recessive condition.

Clearly, not all dwarf breeds are achondroplastic. Yet the converse is also true: not all achondroplastic breeds are dwarves. Brachycephalic achondroplasia shortens just the face of a dog. Because leg-length is unaffected, facially achondroplastic breeds are — all other things being equal — not dwarves. The Boxer, the Dogue de Bordeaux, and the Bullmastiff represent the category of non-dwarf achondroplastics.

Given that brachycephalic achondroplasia, micromelic achondroplasia, and ateliosis all operate independently of each other but not necessarily exclusively of each other in a given individual dog, a scheme of eight possible combinations arises within which all dog breeds can be categorized:

1) brachycephalic achondroplastic/non-ateliotic (e.g., Boxer);
2) brachycephalic achondroplastic/ateliotic (e.g., Boston Terrier);
3) micromelic achondroplastic/non-ateliotic (e.g., Dachshund);
4) micromelic achondroplastic/ateliotic (e.g., Miniature Dachshund);
5) brachycephalic + micromelic achondroplastic/ non-ateliotic (e.g., Bulldog);
6) brachycephalic + micromelic achondroplastic/ ateliotic (e.g., Pug);
7) non-achondroplastic/non-ateliotic (e.g., German Shepherd Dog);
8) non-achondroplastic/ateliotic (e.g., Chihuahua).

Actually, two topologically distinct brachycephalic achondroplasias are inferred to operate in dogs. One form of brachycephalic achondroplasia specifically inhibits the chondrification of Meckel's cartilage in the first visceral arch and so shortens the lower jaw (the *mandible*). The other form of brachycephalic achondroplasia inhibits membranous ossification at the anterior and posterior basicranial epiphyseal growth plate sites and so shortens just the upper face and upper jaw (the *maxillary* region). When mandibular shortening is slight, maxillary achondroplasia results in the strongly undershot under jaw (*mandibular prognathism*) that characterizes the modern English Bulldog, the Boxer, and the Dogue de Bordeaux.

Yet milder forms of mandibular prognathism occur chronically as undesirable aberrations in all dog breeds with achondroplastic heads. The failure of many generations of breeders to eliminate recurrent structural disharmony between opposing jaws in these breeds — together with the highly heterogeneous jaw configurations recorded in the second filial generations of Charles Stockard's extensive hybridization experiments with achondroplastic dog breeds reported in *The Genetic and Endocrinic Basis for Differences in Form and Behavior* (1941) — demonstrate that mandibular achondroplasia and maxillary achondroplasia are essentially separate disorders, each under independent genetic determination. The implication is that the flat-faced dog breeds (such as the Brussels Griffon) in fact evince a *double achondroplasia* — both maxillary and mandibular achondroplasias at once.

Our most completely achondroplastic dog breeds are the toy imports of East Asian origin: the Pekingese, the Shih Tzu, and the Pug. To avoid having always to refer to this group as the "brachycephalic + micromelic achondroplastic/ateliotic dogs" in subsequent chapters, we coin the shorthand: "FAD dogs" (short for "facially achondroplastic dwarf"). The body-forms of these *triply achondroplastic* breeds represent the simultaneous superposition of all three varieties of achondroplasia — micromelic, maxillary, and mandibular — all on a midget frame. Thus, the Pug's disproportionately stumpy legs, tending to bow (*genu varum*), result from micromelic achondroplasia. The Pug's bulging forehead (*frontal bossing*); large, starting eyes (*exophthalmos*); pronounced stop (*recessed nasion*); and short midface (*midface hypoplasia*) all reflect maxillary achondroplasia. The Pug's short lower jaw expresses mandibular achondroplasia. The Pug's extraordinarily flat face and crowded dentition are accidents of the simultaneous operation of maxillary and mandibular achondroplasia.

Although achondroplastic dwarfism probably occurs at characteristic frequencies in all higher animal species, it tends to be naturally selected only under extraordinary circumstances of biogeographical insularity. On the other hand, achondroplastic dwarf races have been developed by artificial selection in virtually all species of domesticated animal: dog, cat, horse, cow, buffalo, pig, sheep, goat, rabbit, and chicken.

Achondroplasia — the most common variety of dwarfism in man — occurs in all human populations at a fairly constant frequency of about 1 in every 26,000 births. Human achondroplasia is readily diagnosed by an definite set of extreme somatic expressions that are remarkably similar in character to those of the FAD dog breeds, such as the Pug. Like the Pug's, the limbs of the human achondroplastic dwarf are shortened by rhizomelic micromelia and tend to *genu varum*. Like the Pug's, the head of the human achondroplastic dwarf exhibits frontal bossing; exophthalmos; recessed nasion; midface hypoplasia; pug nose; respiratory stenosis; malocclusion; and crowded dentition.

Although human achondroplastic dwarves and Pugs show these surprisingly strong external (*phenotypic*) resemblances, they differ fundamentally in the manner in which their respective achondroplasias are genetically determined and transmitted (that is, in their *genotypes*). In the first place, human achondroplastic dwarves inherit both micromelia of the limbs and facial shortening as a unitary syndrome; whereas — as we have seen — Pugs inherit micromelia of the limbs, maxillary shortening, and mandibular shortening as separate and independent traits. In the second place, human achondroplasia is transmitted as a dominant condition with complete penetrance; whereas each of the three localized achondroplasias operative in the Pug breed is transmitted as a dominant condition with incomplete penetrance. In the third place, human achondroplastic dwarves display normal trunk dimensions; whereas Pugs display the miniature trunk dimensions of the ateliotic dwarf.

Let us enlarge our consideration of each of these three contrasts in achondroplastic style to dogs in general. We look first at the species contrast between achondroplasia as a singular syndrome in human beings and as a manifold of separable traits in dogs. In 1994, several research groups reported the unique cause of human achondroplasia to be a point mutation on the distal region of the short arm of chromosome 4, such that arginine is substituted for glycine in a single nucleotide in the transmembrane domain of the gene called Fibroblast Growth Factor Receptor 3 (FGFR3). This gene encodes the growth factor receptors that regulate cartilage growth plate differentiation. The arginine substitution (Arg 380) disrupts signal transduction through FGFR 3 so that

bones develop dystrophically at the epiphyseal growth plate sites. According to the research groups, this single misscripted amino acid determines all the physical manifestations of achondroplasia in human beings.

Even though the chromosomal loci for achondroplasia in dogs have yet to be pinpointed, we may predict that the biochemical etiology of canine achondroplasia will not prove as simple as reported in the human case. Biochemists working in the Dog Genome project at the University of California at Berkeley regard as plausible the hypothesis that an analogous point mutation in FGFR3 will eventually be found to determine achondroplasia in dogs. But recall the several, highly localized achondroplastic effects that we see variously combined in the gamut of achondroplastic dog breeds: the Dachshund with its achondroplastic legs but normal head; the Boxer with its achondroplastic upper jaw but normal legs; the Boston Terrier with its achondroplastic upper jaw, achondroplastic lower jaw, but normal legs; the English Bulldog with its achondroplastic upper jaw and achondroplastic legs; and, most perfectly, the Pug with its achondroplastic upper jaw, achondroplastic lower jaw, and achondroplastic legs.

Separability of traits in expression implies independence of transmission. The Pug's achondroplasia must be the result of at least three separate genetic defects. In respect of dwarfing as of so many other physical characteristics, the 78 chromosomes of *Canis familiaris* would appear to harbor a richer diversity of potential somatic expression than the 46 chromosomes of *Homo sapiens*.

An alternative interpretation, however, is suggested by the occurrence in human populations of a rarer disproportionate dwarfism called *pseudoachondroplasia*. The pseudoachondoplastic dwarf has micromelic limbs but a normal face and skull. The separability of micromelia in expression allows that the Arg 380 point mutation reported in 1994 might be a necessary but not sufficient cause of human achondroplasia. In other words, the reported mutation might determine either micromelic achondroplasia or facial achondroplasia rather than both as a unitary syndrome. If some other point mutation is eventually found to be epistatically linked to the Arg 380 mutation as a cofactor in human achondroplasia, then the chromosomal templates for human

and canine achondroplasias might prove in the future to be somewhat more analogous than they now appear.

We turn to the second contrast between human and canine achondroplastics: Just as the genetic controls on achondroplasia are less simple in dogs than in human beings, so the modes of inheritance are more complex in dogs. Human achondroplasia is transmitted as a *dominant condition with complete penetrance*. *Dominance* here means that if an individual carries the Arg 380-mutation in his genotype, he will be an achondroplastic dwarf in his phenotype. *Complete penetrance* means that the phenotype of an individual who is heterozygous for the Arg 380-mutation (that is, one of whose two homologous FGFR3-genes is mutated by arginine-substitution) will be as symptomatically achondroplastic as that of a homozygous individual (that is, both of whose FGFR3-genes are so mutated). In terms of heritability, these conditions translate into simple probabilities: if both human parents are heterozygous achondroplastic dwarves, then — on average — 75% of their progeny will be achondroplastic dwarves and 25% will be normal in phenotype.

By contrast, none of the three achondroplasias found in dogs is transmitted as a dominant condition with complete penetrance. Micromelic achondroplasia in dogs is transmitted as a dominant condition with *incomplete penetrance*; meaning that a dog whose genotype is heterozygous for the micromelic mutation will have distinctly longer legs than its homozygous dwarf sibling. In terms of heritability, if both dog parents are heterozygous for the micromelic mutation in their genotypes, then — on average — 25% of their progeny will be micromelic achondroplastic dwarves in phenotype; 50% will show intermediate leg-length; and 25% will show normal leg-length.

The mode of inheritance of the brachycephalic achondroplasias in dogs is more complicated still. As we have noted, Stockard's cross-breeding experiments demonstrated that — to a first order of approximation — mandibular and maxillary achondroplasias are transmitted independently in dogs. Like micromelic achondroplasia, each of the two brachycephalic achondroplasias is transmitted as a dominant condition with incomplete penetrance. But Stockard's experiments also demonstrated that — compared to micromelic achondroplasia — the brachycephalic achondroplasias show less statistical regularity and more morphological variability in their modes of inheritance. Stockard inferred that some chemical linkage must mediate between the distinct genetic loci for maxillary and mandibular achondroplasia, enabling some degree of second-order (*epistatic*) interaction between the two sites.

The third and final contrast between human and canine achondroplasias that we consider is that only the latter may be overprinted by ateliosis. Standard Dachshunds, for example, are dwarfed in stature by micromelic achondroplasia; apart from their limbs, they are normal in size. Notwithstanding their achondroplastic dwarfism, Standard Dachshund populations also throw ateliotic dwarves at a low but definite frequency. In the past century, ateliolitic Dachshunds have been deliberately preserved and interbred in order to establish a distinct sub-breed for show — the Miniature Dachshund.

Every Pug is doubly dwarfed just like the Miniature Dachshund. You will never see a dwarf version of a Pug — for the simple reason that every Pug is already both an achondroplastic and ateliotic dwarf. We have already noted that canine achondroplasias are transmitted as dominant conditions with incomplete penetrance; and that canine ateliosis is transmitted as a recessive condition. Consequently, if an individual were heterozygous with respect to either condition, its progeny would necessarily be mixed in phenotype. But Pug is a breed: Pugs bred to Pugs always throw Pugs. Since 100% of Pug progeny are both achondroplastic and ateliotic in phenotype, all Pugs are homozygotes with respect to both achondroplasia and ateliosis.

China Doll

"In the West there was a Buddha named Mañjusri who was always accompanied by a small happa dog and who traveled the four continents as a simple priest… In the heavens the happa dog transformed into a mighty lion with the Buddha riding on his back."

— Tibetan "Yuan Liu" Ching

All modern authorities agree that the Pug originated in China as the short-haired counterpart to the predominantly long-haired facially achondroplastic dwarf (FAD) lap dogs that were bred within the Imperial City in Peking. The earliest historical evidence we have of the Pug is pictorial and comes from around the turn of the eighteenth century. An illustration of a lap dog that exhibits several essential Pug characterisics appears in the Imperial Dog Book by Tsou Yi-Kwei, who served as Vice-Minister of the Board of Rites during the reign of K'ang-hsi (1661–1722), the second emperor of the Manchu dynasty (1644–1911). This lap dog resembles the modern Pug in respect of its achondroplastic face and legs, short dorsal hair, and curled tail. It differs from the modern Pug, however, in respect of its long ventral hair and particolored ("flowered") coat.

The first historical evidence we find of a Chinese lap dog that registers the full syndrome of Pug characteristics — including the uniformly short-haired, self-colored coat — is plastic and comes from the middle of the eighteenth century. A pair of porcelain figurines dating to the reign of Ch'ien-lung (1735–96), the fourth emperor of the Manchu dynasty, clearly represent sejant Pugs. These proto-Pugs — on display at Saltram House in Devon, England — do not differ essentially from the modern Pug except in being somewhat longer in the leg. Significantly, eighteenth-century European Pugs were similarly leggy.

Not until the Tao-kuang period (1820–1850), however, do we learn from written sources the Chinese name for the Pug: *Lo-sze ba-erh*. *Ba-erh* means "lap dog;" *Lo-sze* has the non-literal significance of "short-coated." To situate the *Lo-sze ba-erh* in the Chinese taxonomy of lap dogs requires that we hack our way through a thicket of densely overlapping Chinese terms — upon which hang the bleached bones of many a hapless Pug-writer. Our Vergil through this dark wood shall be V.F.W. Collier in his magisterial study, *Dogs of China and Japan in Nature and Art* (1921). Several synonyms were available in Chinese by the nineteenth century with which to refer to "lap dogs" in general (irrespective of face- or coat-length): *ba-erh*, in vernacular Chinese; *hah-bah* (often transliterated as *happa*), in aristocratic Manchu; and dogs of *Fu-lin*, in classical literary Chinese. For FAD lap dogs in particular, two synonyms existed in nineteenth-century Chinese: *Pen-lo ba-erh* ("lump-forehead lap dog"), in vernacular Chinese; or *Shih-tzu ba-erh* ("lion lap dog"), in literary Chinese.

In vernacular Chinese, the class of "lump-forehead lap dogs" was itself partitioned into three types according to coat-length. The first type was characterized by very long, flowing hair and was called *Shih-tzu ba-erh* (note that this vernacular usage is more restrictive than the literary usage mentioned above). Soon after the collapse of the Manchu dynasty, this type made its first appearance in England — where it took the name "Shih Tzu."

The second type of "lump-forehead lap dog" was characterized by short hair and was called (as noted above) *Lo-sze ba-erh*. The leggier form of this type that prevailed during the early Manchu dynasty had been familiar to the English as the "Pug" ever since the early eighteenth century. As booty of the sack of the Imperial City and the Old Summer Palace by British troops in 1860 at the conclusion of the Second Opium War, the squat nineteenth-century version of the *Lo-sze ba-erh* was smuggled into England, where it in turn took Victorian Pugdom by storm. By the time of the founding of the Pug Dog Club of England in 1881, the squat new *Lo-sze ba-erh* had quite supplanted its leggier throwback in English breeding circles. The newcomer from Peking usurped the name of "Pug" as smoothly as its predecessor had once usurped the same name from its own simian predecessor (see Chapter 6).

The third — and foremost — type of "lump-forehead lap dog" was characterized by long, somewhat tufty hair and was called either *Ba-erh Kou* ("small-dog dog") or *happa* (note that this vernacular usage is more restrictive than the aristocratic Manchu usage mentioned above). By the mid-nineteenth century, *happa* had evolved into a portmanteau term embracing six strains of lap dog that had been separately distinguished in the early nineteenth century.

The *happa* was far and away the dominant type of Chinese lap dog — of which the *Shih-tzu ba-erh* and *Lo-sze ba-erh* were considered to be minor offshoots. Spirited out of the Imperial City by the same depredatory agency as the *Lo-sze ba-erh*, the *happa* was rechristened the "Pekingese" in England. We shall

henceforth freely anglicize the long-coated *happa* to "Pekingese;" the short-coated *Lo-sze ba-erh* to "Chinese Pug;" and the generic *Pen-lo ba-erh* to "FAD dog."

No artistic representations of the Pekingese predating those of the Chinese Pug are known to exist. That is to say, FAD dogs can be positively linked only China's last dynasty — the Manchu. The FAD dog cult reached its zenith during the boom times of the Tao-kuang period (1820–1850). It lingered thereafter through the long death agonies of the Manchu dynasty thanks to the zealous patronage of Tz'u-hsi — the so-called "Empress Dowager" who ferociously contrived to control the state affairs of China from 1861 until her death in 1908.

So archconservative that she gloried in the sobriquet of "Old Buddha," the Empress Dowager balked at nothing in eliminating challenges to her supremacy. She made a succession of child emperors her prisoners; she executed reformers en masse; and she unleashed the full fury of the Boxer Rebellion in 1900 by ordering her subjects to slaughter all foreigners and Chinese Christians. It was upon the breeding program of the Imperial kennels half a century earlier that Tz'u-hsi had first demonstrated her formidable micromanagement skills while still a low-ranking concubine of the Hsien-feng emperor (reigned 1850–61). She began the practice of docking the tails of FAD dogs in order to enhance their resemblance to the Buddhist spirit-lion (*Fu*) and its less spiritually exalted cousin, the lion-dog (*Fu* dog) — both omnipresent motifs in Chinese art since the arrival of Buddhism in the first century AD. She also fostered the breeding of special new FAD strains for certain physical nuances susceptible of interpretation as Buddhist religious symbols or marks of imperial rank.

The "Old Buddha" later oversaw the production of Imperial Dog Books that prescribed in picture and poetic "pearls" not only the distinctions amongst her many varieties of Pekingese dogs but also the points of similarity and difference between the Pekingese and the Chinese Pug as they stood in the latter nineteenth century. Both Pekingese and Chinese Pug should mimic the mythical *Fu* in certain essential features: compact, well-knit body; flat, "knife-cut" face; square jaw; and deep-cleft, double-looped nose outline. This last feature was prized for its simultaneous evocation of three religious symbols: the Buddhist scepter-emblem, *Ru-yi*; the Chinese radical for "cloud;" and the Lotus sign (one of the thirty-two *laksanas* or "Superior Marks of Buddha").

In contrast to the Pekingese, however, the Chinese Pug should have a much shorter coat and much looser skin in order to pucker its brow into a multiplex of deep wrinkles. Moreover, a precise configuration of these forehead wrinkles was sought: three horizontal creases bisected by one vertical. This configuration was perceived as replicating the Chinese character *yu* — one of whose meanings is "imperial ruler." This "prince mark" was commonly carved on the foreheads of statuary *Fu* dogs — as befitted familiars of one of the celestial manifestations of Prince Buddha.

The Empress Dowager was the last exponent of a Chinese imperial cult of the lap dog that stretched back some two millenia. The first attested reference to the oldest generic Chinese term for "small dog" comes from the *Shuo-wen* dictionary (*c.* 100 AD), which defines *pai* (or *bai*) as "a dog with short legs." The *Kuang-yün* dictionary of 1007 defines *pai* both as "a dog with a short head" and as "an under-table dog" (the latter implying very short legs). Although none of these definitions — nor any other independent evidence — warrants the inference that the *pai* was a FAD, they do plainly connote a lap dog.

A named but undescribed variety of *pai* makes an historical appearance in AD 732, when a Korean state included a *Sichuan pai* as part of its tribute to Japan. Another *pai* type called the *Lo-chiang bai* first appears *c.* AD 990. It is possible that the *Lo-chiang* dog is related to the *Sichuan pai*, insofar as Lo-Chiang is a sub-prefecture thirty miles north of Chengtu, capital of Sichuan province. The *Lo-chiang bai* in question was named Tao-hua ("Peach Flower") and hailed from Ho-chow (200 miles east of Lo-chiang). This *Lo-chiang bai* was "extremely small" and attended the T'ai-tsung Emperor everywhere, preceding him with monitory barks. When the Emperor died in AD 998, Tao-hua reportedly died of sorrow and was buried by imperial decree in an umbrella alongside his master. No cause is given to infer that the *Lo-chiang bai* was either a FAD or short-coated. Indeed, the second mention of the *Lo-chiang bai* — which occurs in reference to an imperial watchdog installed during a mutiny of palace soldiers in AD 1041 — would seem to suggest otherwise.

Collier makes an etymological argument that the nineteenth-century *Lo-sze ba-erh* and the tenth-century *Lo-chiang bai* might be one and the same beast. Given that *sze* is a common Sichuan place-name suffix, Collier urges that it is possible there once existed a variant form of *Lo-chiang*: namely, *Lo-chiang-sze**. If this hypothetical form were then contracted by dropping *-chiang-*, modern *Lo-sze* would be generated. (V. F. W. Collier was so fond of the game of generating new names from old names that he fiddled with his own name, which was actually W. F. C. Collins.)

Absent any other less conjectural information, Collier's argument must be accounted very wobbly — for several reasons. First, both steps in his argument are hypothetical. Second, almost a millenium separates the last mention of the *Lo-chiang bai* and the first mention of the *Lo-sze ba-erh*. Third, the only word known in modern Sichuan for "lap dog" is *Ching-kou* ("Peking dog"). Finally, even if etymological descent from *Lo-chiang bai* to *Lo-sze ba-erh* could be proved, it would not necessarily imply biological descent. Any attempt to derive our modern FAD Pug from a putative tenth-century Sichuan ancestor must fall foul of a hard fact of pre-Manchu dynasty Chinese cultural history: All representations of natural lap dogs (as opposed to the manifestly mythical, highly conventionalized *Fu* dog images that stood sentinel at temples and in tombs) in Chinese art prior to the Manchu dynasty show long-coated specimens with long muzzles.

The most naturalistic representations of lap dogs before the Manchu dynasty occur in paintings of the Ming dynasty (1368–1644). For example, the exquisite *Dog in the Bamboo Grove* — dating from the reign of the Hsüan-te emperor (1425–35) — depicts a short-legged, long-muzzled lap dog with long, flat, silky hair hanging almost to the ground. Far from being harbingers of the FAD dogs of the Manchu dynasty, the extant images of Ming dynasty dogs much more nearly resemble Malteses in body and especially in face.

The Maltese is an ancient long-haired, long-muzzled toy breed well-attested in the art and literature of peri-Mediterranean civilizations since classical Greek time. Recall the classical Chinese synonym for "lap dog": dog of *Fu-lin*. This word bears no relation to the *Fu* lion-dog. Rather, *Fu-lin* is the Chinese word for "Byzantium;" being a Chinese transliteration of the last word of the Greek phrase, *eis ten polin* ("in the city") — from which Byzantium's Turkish name *Istanbul* is also derived.

The dog of *Fu-lin* receives its first historical mention *c.* AD 980 from Ma-tuan Lin in connection with the Kao-tsu emperor, who reigned AD 618–626. This emperor received from the Turkoman emperor two dogs "born in *Fu-lin*" that were very small (six inches high and one foot long) and very intelligent. Nothing was said in this or any subsequent citation to suggest flattened physiognomy in the dogs of *Fu-lin*.

Trade and embassies were routinely exchanged between the Byzantine and Chinese empires across Turkoman territories between the seventh and fourteenth centuries. Malta belonged to the Byzantine empire from AD 395 to 870. The Maltese dog constituted a premium Byzantine trade and state gift commodity. Every indication — linguistic, artistic, and archival — supports the inference that the dogs of *Fu-lin* were Malteses.

Neither was the *Shih-tzu kou* ("lion dog") a FAD dog prior to the Manchu dynasty. The earliest mention of the *Shih-tzu kou* — dating to AD 1371 and referring to an incident in AD 1131 — concerns a savage temple attack dog. Even after the dawn of the Manchu dynasty, the *Shih-tzu* was apparently still not a FAD. Athanasius Kircher — the Jesuit orientalist (1601–1680) who meticulously digested and published cultural reports filed by the Jesuit world missions — reproduced a portrait of the K'ang-hsi emperor with his dog *c.* 1667. This dog — presumed on independent documentary grounds to be called a *Shih-tzu* — shows a conspicuously long muzzle.

In summary, there is no evidence of FAD lap dogs in China prior to the early Manchu dynasty. On the other hand, there is abundant evidence that virtually all imperial lap dogs during the entire Manchu dynasty (1644–1911) were FADs. In Europe, by contrast, FAD dogs were extremely faddish. In nineteenth-century France, for example — as Kathleen Kete tells us in *The Beast in the Boudoir* (1994) — the Pug was top lap dog of the First Empire (1804–15); but surrendered that primacy successively to miniature spaniels, greyhounds, and terriers before finally returning to vogue again at the end of the century.

Two questions here obtrude. Where did the FAD lap dogs that appeared in Peking in the mid-seventeenth century come from? And why did they henceforth monopolize the court kennels of the Manchu dynasty until its collapse two-and-a-half centuries later? What, in other words, explains the enduring and exclusive bond between FAD dogs and Manchu rulers?

The most plausible answer to the question of provenance is that the Fifth Dalai Lama introduced Tibetan FAD dogs to the Manchu court in 1652. Just two years before the accession of the first emperor of the Manchu dynasty (the Shun-chi emperor, who

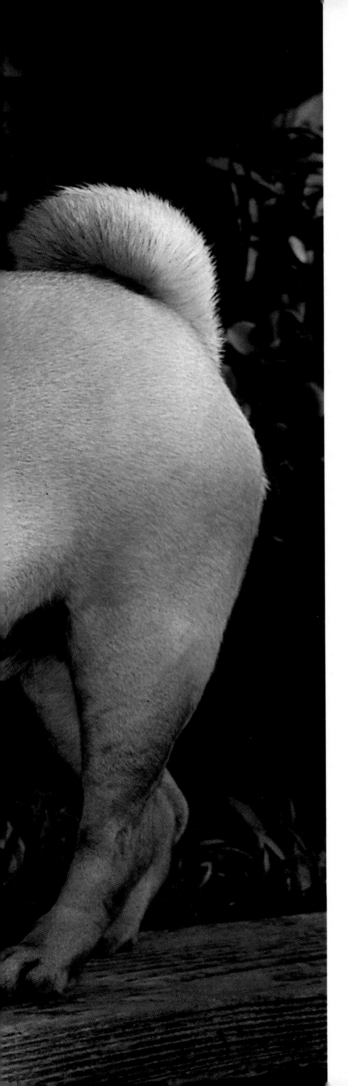

reigned 1644–61), the Fifth Dalai Lama had been enthroned as Tibet's theocratic ruler by the chief of the Khoshut Mongols, who had invaded Tibet in support of the Yellow Hat sect of Tibetan Buddhist monks in their power struggle with the Red Hats. By designating himself the Dalai Lama's military protector, the Mongol chief had heightened the anxieties of the new Manchu emperor concerning the territorial ambitions of the Oryat Mongol tribes on China's western borders.

It behooved the Manchu emperor to offset the Mongol incursion into Tibetan politics by reviving the formal patron-priest relationship between the Chinese emperor and the Tibetan Lama that had flourished during the Mongol dynasty (1206–1368) — as heir to which the upstart Manchu dynasty sought to legitimize itself. No less, it behooved the Dalai Lama to cement such a relationship with the Manchu emperor in order to prevent his own subordination to his self-appointed Mongol protector.

In 1652, consequently, Shun-chi welcomed the Fifth Dalai Lama to Peking for an extended state visit with the fullest honors ever accorded a foreign sovereign by a Chinese emperor. Shun-chi built the Tibetan-style White Dagoba within the Imperial City to house the Dalai Lama's religious exercises during his visit; and the Hindu-style Yellow Pagoda (so called in reference to the Yellow Hat sect) just outside the city walls to accommodate the Dalai Lama, his numerous monastic entourage, and future Grand Lamas of Peking.

Tibetan Buddhism — with its fantastically fluid metaphysical universe populated by teeming systems of celestial and horrific *bodhisattvas* (hierarchical manifestations of the mind of Buddha) whose lurid images dominate its art — appealed to the Manchu sensibility no less than to the Mongol. The Manchu elite was recruited from the most boreal of the Manchu tribes (namely, the Chien-chou tribes), who were — like the Mongols from whom, as Tungids, they were different both ethnically and linguistically — seminomadic semi-pastoralists steeped in shamanistic animism.

No *bodhisattva* was the object of a more popular cult in Tibetan Buddhism than Mañjusri: the celestial *bodhisattva* personifying the transcendental wisdom of the primary Buddha. Mañjusri assumed manifold manifestations. At his most horrific, Mañjusri would sprout nine heads all the better to grimace with while coupling in upright position with his female consort as they trod monsters to pulp. In his more popular image, Mañjusri would take the benign form of a

majestic sky-god holding a book and sword while serenely seated on a celestial, flat-faced spirit-lion.

The Dalai Lama reciprocated the great honor shown him by Shun-chih during the state visit of 1652 by investing him with the honorific title that he so coveted from Buddhist scriptures: *Man Chu Hsi Li* (Mañjusri). This was the big pay-off. Henceforth, the Manchu emperors billed themselves as temporal incarnations of the divine *bodhisattva*. So essential to the legitimation of his dynastic ambitions had Shin-chih's father regarded the identification with Mañjusri that he had changed the name of his northern tribal dynasty from *Chin* to *Manchu* and the name of his own tribal people from *Juchen* to *Manchu*.

Like Mañjusri, his spirit-lion steed could magically mutate at will. During Mañjusri's earthly rovings in the guise of a mild scholar-priest, the mighty lion would assume the humble shape of a brachycephalic lap dog trotting at his master's side. If his master had occasion to demonstrate his true celestial majesty, this little dog would instantly swell into a lion of colossal size and strength.

Within the confines of their labyrinthine monasteries, the Tibetan monks had devoutly bred into existence a strain of FAD "hand" dogs in imitation of the stylized image of Mañjusri's lion-steed. Chinese scholars record that, during the Fifth Dalai lama's state visit, such Tibetan "lion-dogs" were presented to Shun-chih to attend him at court as appurtenances of his new Mañjusri title. Successive Dalai Lamas on state visits to Peking continued the sacred rite of presenting Tibetan "lion-dogs" to Manchu rulers: from the Ch'ienlung emperor (reigned 1735–96) right down to the Empress Dowager in 1908. Westerners privileged to see this last batch of Tibetan "lion-dogs" presented by a Dalai Lama described them as being very similar in appearance to the standard FAD Pekingese "lion-dogs."

We are now in a position to give a concise answer to our second question as to the reason for the enduring and exclusive bond between FAD lap dogs and Manchu rulers. Just as the Manchu emperor was — by declaration of the Dalai Lama — the eponymous incarnation of divine Mañjusri; so the FAD lap dog was — by gift of the Dalai Lama — the temporal incarnation of Mañjusri's spirit-lion. FAD lap dogs figured as permanent fixtures of the imperial court throughout the long Manchu dynasty because they were not just emblems but actual organic projections of the divine power conferred on the emperor by the Dalai Lama. The breeding and possession of FAD lap dogs was therefore an exclusive imperial Manchu prerogative. Anybody outside the imperial household who dared presume upon the emperor's prerogative was summarily put to death.

Barbarian myth reinforced the Buddhist religious bond between the Manchu rulers and their FAD lap dogs. The Juchen people — as the Manchus traditionally called themselves — had dwelt continuously on the Manchurian Plain as a culturally and ethnically distinct population since Neolithic time. They were regarded by their Chinese neighbors to the south as periodically alarming frontier barbarians. Dynastic domination of the vast Chinese population by such a numerically negligible alien people as the Juchen/Manchu depended critically on their leaders' success in permanently converting their full budget of seminomadic manpower into a tightly disciplined standing army of occupation, which was organized into "banners" headquartered in the Imperial City. To keep the corporate integrity of its army and administration from being eroded by ethnic and cultural assimilation, the Manchu elite enacted strict apartheid laws mandating purity of Manchu education and language and prohibiting social intercourse and miscegenation with non-Manchus.

A central element of the Manchu racial ideology so vigorously promoted by the Manchu rulers was the Juchens' canine ancestry myth. As detailed by David White in *Myths of the Dog-Man* (1991), the Juchen believed that they were descended from the union of a white bitch and a man who came down from heaven. They consequently referred to themselves as a race of Dog-Men. To avert epidemics, the Juchen would impale a white dog upon a high pole to act as intermediary between heaven and earth. Straw dogs were shot full of arrows and buried in Juchen graves to conduct the dead to the other world. Chinese words echoed Juchen beliefs. The Chinese ideogram for *Juchen* employed the radical for "dog." The ancient Chinese name for the Manchu homeland was the Kingdom of the Dogs (*Kou kuo*). Juchen selfidentification with the dog can only have enhanced the prestige of the FAD lap dog in the racially purist imperial Manchu court.

The cultural readiness of the Manchu/Juchen to perceive one another as cynomorphic men may well have taken a quietly comic turn. During the Manchu dynasty, two distinct physical strains — today virtually swamped out of existence by a century of intermarriage with the Chinese majority — appear to have

co-existed within the Manchu population. According to the research of Erwin von Baelz (1890), the northern Manchu strain — including the Chien-chou tribes, which supplied the Manchu aristocracy — tended to a narrow face; somewhat aquiline nose; small mouth; and receding chin. This type is exemplified in the naturalistic portrait of the Ch'ien-lung emperor by the Sino-Italian Jesuit painter-priest, Giuseppe Castiglione *aka* Lang Shih-ning (1688-1768).

According to S.M. Shirokogovoff (1923), the other Manchu strain — which supplied the ranks of the Manchu banners and of the emperor's Office of Household — tended to the Buriat type, which displays the most extremely brachycephalic skull dimensions of any human population. William Howells' craniometric analysis in *Skull shapes and the map* (1989) of an archeological sample of Buriat skulls yields the hyperbrachycephalic median cranial index of 109% (recall that any human skull whose width-to-length ratio exceeds 80% is classified as brachycephalic). This second Manchu strain tended to a broad, flat nose; wide-set eyes; and strongly prominent zygomatic arch — together producing an effect of extraordinary facial

flatness. In body, this second Manchu strain tended to be stout, small, broad shouldered, and somewhat bowlegged.

It is not far-fetched to imagine the Manchu emperor and his nobles tacitly sharing a superior amusement at the superficial resemblance between the two species of imperial courtier. The canine courtier was the most brachycephalic (with a cranial index of about 108%) and anthropomorphic of small dogs; the Manchu courtier of the Office of Household was the most brachycephalic (with a cranial index of about 109%) and cynomorphic of small men.

There was a darker resemblance, as well. The Manchu elite valued both FAD lap dogs and hyperbrachycephalic Manchus as props of the imperial throne. For the sake of dynastic stability, the Manchu rulers compelled both sets of their brachycephalic servants by law to inbreed.

Orange Herring

"These dogs were white little hounds, with crooked noses, called Camuses."

— Sir Roger Williams,
The Actions of the Lowe Countries
(ante 1595)

It is the received wisdom in English-speaking Pug-dom that the first documented reference to the Pug breed in Europe dates to 1572, when a legendary little dog played the hero's part in a pivotal event during the revolt of Lutheran Netherlands against Catholic Spain. The assertion that this heroic dog was a Pug — tirelessly repeated and improved by all succeeding generations of Pug-writers in English since it was first advanced in 1858 — is based on an anecdote entitled "The Prince of Orange's Dog," contained in Sir Roger Williams' *The Actions of the Lowe Countries* (written before 1595 but not published until 1618).

The event recounted in the "The Prince of Orange's Dog" took place in September 1572. William I, Prince of Orange and leader of the Dutch revolt, was attempting to relieve his brother Louis of Nassau, whose army lay invested by the Spanish army in the city of Mons (in what is now southern Belgium). On the night of the 11th, the Prince's encampment in nearby Harmignies was surprised in its sleep and overrun by a stealthy Spanish sally or *camisado* (so called because the raiding soldiers wore *camisas* or shirts over their armor to identify each other in the dark — no... not because they were trying to catch *camuses*). The Prince had just enough time to jump on his horse and escape the carnage closing about him thanks to a little dog in his tent that had awakened him at the first alarm by scratching and crying and leaping on his master's face.

But for this dog, some have argued, established Protestantism would have been defeated in both Holland and England. For without the dog, William of Orange would have been killed; without William, the Dutch revolt would have failed; and without Dutch independence, William III would not have been available as the Protestant champion to replace James II on the British throne. The breed that can claim this little sentinel as its own has much to boast.

Now, the primary evidence for identifying the breed of the Dog Who Saved Protestantism as a Pug is the description offered by Sir Roger Williams in 1618: "For truth, ever since [1572], untill the Prince's dying day [1584], he kept one of that dog's race; so did many of his friends and followers. The most or all of these dogs were white **little hounds**, with **crooked noses**, called **Camuses**" [emphases ours].

Our classic authorities on the Pug — such as Wilhelmina Swainston-Goodger — base their deduction that these "little white hounds" were in fact Pugs on two considerations. First, they point out that *camus* is a French word meaning "flat-nosed" or "pug-nosed." Second, they maintain that the Pug was ever after honored as the court mascot of the House of Orange: originally in Holland; then — upon the accession of William III of Orange (grandson of the William of our story) to the British throne in the Glorious Revolution of 1688–9 — in England, too. These authorities further note that the eagerness of the successive King Georges of eighteenth-century England to advertise their anti-Catholic credentials led them to perpetuate the Orangist Court Pug in the guise of their own Hanoverian Court Pug. The clincher proving beyond a reasonable doubt that the Prince of Orange's famous Camus was indeed a Pug was clarioned by Estelle Ross in *The Book of Noble Dogs* (1924): "One thing is certain: from that day forward the Prince was never without a pug on his bed; and where he sleeps in effigy in Delft Cathedral one lies at his feet." Ross even gives us the name of this illustrious Pug: Pompey.

At first blush, the cumulative effect of this mass of circumstantial evidence would seem to confirm beyond a reasonable doubt the argument for the Pug. Closer inspection, however, discloses a house of cards. For some of the evidence turns out to be unsupported; some to be subtly wrong; and the rest to be blatantly wrong. Let us start with the faultiest grade of evidence: the blatantly wrong. Such is the statement that the sculpted dog at the feet of William of Orange's "effigy in Delft Cathedral" represents a Pug.

The marble mausoleum of William of Orange in Delft's Nieuwe Kerk ("New Church") was installed in 1614–21 and stands as the crowning masterpiece of Hendrick de Keyser (1565–1621), the greatest Dutch sculptor of the time and a skilled exponent of naturalism. Concerning the breed of the sculpted dog, we have been generously supplied with eye-witness reports both by dog fanciers living in Delft (Dirk Bazuin and Bert Vortman) and by an officer of the Netherlands' national Pug club, delightfully named

Commedia (Gerda Broekkamp, a Commedia judge and board member). The word from Holland is unanimous and unequivocal: Keyser's little dog is a Kooikerhondje.

The Kooikerhondje is a small (20-24 lb) white hound with bright orange markings that is virtually unknown outside its native Holland. The Kooiker breed was developed to assist hunters by driving half-tame decoy ducks under a type of fowling net (*kooi*) set on canal banks to trap wild ducks. In Holland, it is the Kooiker that is universally credited with having been the Dog Who Saved the Prince and so the mascot of the House of Orange. A recent Dutch made-for-television film biography of William of Orange, for example, casts a Kooiker in the role for the *camisado* scene.

Dutch unanimity for the Kooiker can hardly surprise us once we learn that it is grounded on the Dutch national epic. In a personal communication, Mrs Broekkamp points out that the story of the Harmignies *camisado* is fully recounted in *Nederlandse historiën* (first published in 1642) — the magisterial history of the Dutch rebellion by the most brilliant writer of the Dutch Renaisance, Pieter Corneliszoon Hooft. In twenty volumes costing him nineteen years of literary labor, Hooft chronicled William of Orange's heroic struggle for Dutch independence from 1555 to 1585. According to Hooft's account, the Dog Who Saved the Prince was a Kooiker named Kuntze. Dutch people today are apt to be wryly amused when they are informed that the English-speaking fancy across the Channel has cavalierly re-assigned Kuntze's cherished role in their national foundation myth to a Pug named Pompey.

As it turns out, Ross recycled the name "Pompey" from an 1856 version of the *camisado* story as freely re-told by an amateur American historian named John Motley. His novelistically embroidered history, *The Rise of the Dutch Republic*, identifies Pompey as a "spaniel." Motley apparently selected the name "Pompey" for its generic sense of "lap-dog," which in turn derived from a popular satirical biography of a small spaniel, entitled *The History of Pompey the Little: or the Life and Adventures of a Lap-Dog*. This runaway bestseller by the Reverend Francis Coventry ran through many editions in the decades following its first publication in 1751. The title is, of course, a jocular play on the epithet of Caesar's rival, Pompey the Great.

Having exposed the blatantly wrong evidence, let us downshift to the next grade of faulty evidence offered in support of the proposition that the Dog Who Saved the Prince was a Pug: namely, unsupported evidence. Under this rubric falls the statement that the Pug enjoyed a special status vis-à-vis the House of Orange. For there seems, in truth, to be no contemporary documentary evidence from the seventeenth century to indicate that the Pug was an Orange mascot. Rather, the first references to such a special status appear to come from the pens of writers in Victorian England two centuries later.

What is more, diligent search of Dutch art of the seventeenth century reveals no images of Pugs at all. Wim Jansen — chairman of Commedia; esteemed breeder of Pugs under the kennel-name, *Empereur Napoleon*; noted connoisseur and collector of Pug art — knows of no representation of the Pug in Dutch art prior to the eighteenth century. As a matter of fact, the first representations of the European Pug are found not in seventeenth-century Dutch art but in eighteenth-century French and English painting (*see below*). Kooikers, on the other hand, are depicted in scores of paintings (including portraits of members of the House of Orange) by seventeenth-century Dutch masters — most notably, Jan Steen and Jan Vermeer.

Into our final grade of faulty evidence — the subtly wrong — falls the identification of Sir Roger Williams' sixteenth-century *Camuses* with our modern *Pugs*. Now it is quite true that the adjective *camus* in modern French is accurately translated into modern English as "pug-nosed." (Contributing to Albert Camus' existential estrangement was the comic ring of his name to the French ear.) It is moreover true that *camuso* is a rare synonym of *carlino* in modern Italian. But it constitutes an error of anachronism to infer from these modern equivalences that the noun *Camus* in sixteenth-century English must therefore have meant "Pug-dog."

Cognate words in different languages mutate at different rates. It is folly to extrapolate a definition for an obsolete sixteenth-century English word from a cognate word in a modern foreign language based

on the latter's modern English equivalent. Suppose, for example, you come across the obsolete word *fusil* in a sixteenth-century English text. You know that the modern French word *fusil* means "rifle" or "shotgun." Can you infer that sixteenth-century English *fusil* meant "rifle" or "shotgun?"

No! For one thing, neither the rifle nor the shotgun had even been invented in the sixteenth century. For another, it so happens that in sixteenth-century English *fusil* meant "a fire steel for a tinder box." The only acceptable way to get at the actual meaning of an obsolete sixteenth-century word is to look at the actual occurrences of that word in sixteenth-century texts.

Similar considerations apply to the sixteenth-century English word *Camus*. For one thing, *pug-nosed* (the English definition of the modern French word *camus*) is a word that did not come into existence until the nineteenth century. For another, *camus* in the sixteenth century was already a venerable English word, the precise meaning of which was distinct from the "pug-nosed" of modern French *camus*. Middle English *camus* was probably not even derived not from Medieval French, but rather from Gaelic *camus*, meaning "bay" or "concavity." (More remotely, this Gaelic word may in turn be related to Greek *simos*, meaning both "concavity" and "snub nose." In the latter sense, it supplied the root of modern English *simian*.)

In sixteenth-century English, *Camus* meant "a person or animal with a *camus* nose," where *camus* meant "of a nose, curved upward or downward." This sense is made clear in the following OED citations [emphases added]: *Nose some dele* **hoked**, *And* **camously croked** (1528); *A* **camoise** *nose, that is to say,* **crooked** *vpwarde as the Morians* (1580); *This slut with a* **cammoysed haucks** *nose* (1583); *The former have* **flat** *noses, the other are hooked and* **camoise** *nosed vpward* (1601). In these four citations, note that a camus nose might be either hooked downward like a hawk's, or crooked upward like a Moor's; that the camus nose is explicitly contrasted to the flat nose; and, finally, that *crooked* in conjunction with *camus* means "concavely curved."

With these points in mind, we can now elucidate Sir Roger William's key phrase — *white little hounds, with* **crooked** *noses, called* **camuses.** What is described here are clearly not flat-nosed dogs such as our modern Pugs. Rather,

we are looking at dogs with concavely curved noses — that is, showing in profile a distinct concave angular break or "stop." (In her thoughtful study *Toy Dogs and their Ancestors* published in 1911, Mrs. Neville Lytton — great-granddaughter of that romantic champion of the dog, Lord Byron — proposed with regard to the phrase in question that "The crooked nose may merely mean stop." Due consideration of the citations above confirm her proposal.) But the Pug has the flattest nose in the dogdom — not a stop. The Kooikerhondje, on the other hand, shows a such a pronounced stop that its nose is often somewhat dished.

A last remark on Sir Roger Williams' key phrase is warranted: *little hounds* can describe Kooikers, but not Pugs. In *A Treatise of Englishe Dogges* (1576, Fleming's translation), the Cambridge University physician Dr Johannes Caius definitively states: *Hound signifieth such a dog only as serveth to hunt.* The Pug is certainly no hunter… well, he might put a move on a sluggish fly if he thinks there might be a laugh in it. The Kooiker, on the other hand, is an expert duck-hunter.

We have shown that the preponderance of evidence points to the Kooikerhondje as being the Dog Who Saved Protestantism. Yet an obvious objection immediately presents itself: Why on earth would Victorian English writers even bother to plug a Pug into a old Dutch story featuring a patriotic Kooiker? The answer depends on the resurgent popularity of the Pug in Victorian England; the initial popularity of the Pug in Georgian England; and a failure to appreciate a little joke.

The Pug breed first came into vogue in England during the mid-eighteenth century; fell into comparative disfavor shortly after the turn of the century; and then resurged in popularity in the mid-nineteenth century. The new breed of Victorian dog writers catered to the social pretensions of the new bourgeois dog fancy by constructing long and impressive historical pedigrees for the most fashionable pure breeds. After an Englishman named Edward Rimbault stumbled onto Sir Roger William's dusty anecdote in 1858 and queried publicly in the periodical *Notes and Queries* whether Sir Roger's *Camus* might not be a Pug, dog writers such as "Stonehenge" in 1867, "Idstone" in 1872, and Rawdon Lee in 1894 were ready to make the most of the suggestion. They already knew that the Pug first

appeared in English language and art in the second quarter of the eighteenth century; that King George III and Queen Charlotte had Pugs in their dog entourage in the latter part of the eighteenth century; and that an eighteenth-century synonym for Pug was *Dutch Mastiff*. To this information they added the new notion that the Pug had been the mascot of the House of Orange since 1572.

Everything fit. Like a vision, the pedigree of the European Pug suddenly stretched back down the royal road from Queen Victoria, through the three King George's and William III of England, to William I of Orange. And the bonus twist to the story was a true bonanza: if it were not for that first Pug that saved William I, England would never have traveled the royal road leading to Victoria and world dominion. Phew!

The story makes stirring copy but fake history. We have already refuted the Pug's claim to be the ancient mascot of the House of Orange. Neither is there any evidence that the Pug thereafter became the mascot of the House of Hanover. Wihelmina Swainston-Goodger asserts that the portrait of George III at Hampton Court (painted by Peter Eduard Ströhling in 1807) shows him with his Pug. This painting in fact depicts a small spaniel that looks nothing like a Pug. It is by no means implausible that Pugs may have figured in George III's menagerie, but they would have been there for the simple reason that the Pug was a chic breed in both England and Germany. As for Queen Victoria, she did have an horripilatingly ugly Pug in her kennels in 1854 — but during her long reign she never met a dog she didn't like amongst the hundreds that she owned. The final element in the Victorian Pug-myth is a little tricky: What about *Dutch Mastiff*? At the very least, this synonym surely implies that the Pug came to England from Holland!

Not necessarily. Recall that England and the Dutch Republic were bitter commercial adversaries who engaged one another in three hotly contended naval wars in the second half of the seventeenth century. The Dutch gave as good as they got — once prostrating English sea-pride by burning the English fleet at anchor near London. In the seventeeth century, the English learned to fear as well as to detest their Dutch co-religionists.

In the eighteenth century, however, the growth of English power so far outstripped the Dutch that by

the Fourth Anglo-Dutch War during the American revolution, the Dutch Republic could not even assemble a proper fleet. A whole family of tongue-in-cheek oxymorons arose in eighteenth-century English to insult the prostrated rival, lately so feared: *Dutch courage*, *Dutch treat*, *Dutch defense*, etc. *Dutch mastiff* belongs to this family: it lampoons Dutch harmlessness in the same way that *Dutch treat* lampoons Dutch niggardliness. In these sarcastic expressions, *Dutch* was deployed simply as a general qualifier meaning "not really." To infer that the qualified entity is peculiarly Dutch in origin is to miss completely the defamatory humor.

A case in point is *Dutch-buttocked cattle*. This strain of cattle was selectively bred in the late eighteenth century for humongous bubble-butts. May it be inferred that this steatopygous breed originated in the Netherlands? No way, Hans. As a matter of fact, it was a group of farmers in Yorkshire who created and grinningly named the *Dutch-buttocked* breed. By the same token, it is no less reckless to infer from the expression *Dutch mastiff* that the European Pug originated in Holland.

The old English zest for sending up the Dutch national character lives on to this day in popular English culture. The 1995 English movie *England, My England* depicts William III not as the dignified and able European prince that he conspicuously was — but as an unkempt buffoon given to spasmodic tics, insane cackles, and deviant bedroom habits. After studying a succession of grotesque grimaces on William's idiot face, where does the English camera pan? — to the faces of three little Pugs at his feet!

As a matter of fact, there appears to be no hard contemporary evidence of the presence of Pugs in England prior to 1730. Identifications of Pugs in two earlier English paintings seem to have been mistaken. In his companion book to a 1996 exhibition at the National Gallery in London, Alistair Lang identifies as a "Dutch mastiff" the dog portrayed in an English painting entitled *Old Virtue* that is dated to about 1702. The painting in question is of a dog named Virtue and hangs in Dunham Massey, a National House west of Manchester. This Cheshire dog is

enigmatical: he looks a bit like a Pug, but then he doesn't.

A tally of Virtue's Pug-like features, however, discloses their essential un-Puggishness: his trunk is barrel-shaped — but heavy and smooth rather than cobby and rolled; his coat is short — but brindled rather than self-colored; his tail is lank rather than curled; his legs are wide set — but long; his eyes are wide set — but small; his head is wrinkled — but only longitudinally and only on the forehead; his muzzle is short — but still pronounced. These are all mastiff features. What we have here is not a Pug, but an overfed, crop-eared Mastiff well past his prime.

Virtue was old when he posed for his portrait. He died soon thereafter and was buried under an elaborate monument at Dunham Massey which survives to this day. The portrait is unsigned. Alistair Lang identifies the self-effacing portraitist as either Leendert Knyff (1650–1722) or Jan Wyck (1652–1700). That both these candidates were Dutch expatriates (Jan Wyck accompanied William III to Ulster in 1688, where he painted scenes of the Battle of Boyne) may have suggested to Lang that Old Virtue was one of the storied invasion of "Dutch mastiffs" during the Glorious Revolution. An exhumation of Old Virtue's skeleton would be desirable in order to settle the question.

East of Manchester, in ducal Chatsworth House, hangs an even earlier painting that has been mooted to depict a Pug. This painting is the portrait done in 1698 by Sir Godfrey Kneller of the 3rd Earl of Burlington, lording it over his sisters on his fourth birthday. One of the Earl's little sisters cradles a very tiny short-haired dog that Ellen Brown — Historian of the The Pug Dog Club of Britain — tentatively identifies in *The Complete Pug* (1997) as a Pug. This identification seems doubtful. For even though the dog is so tiny as to be a newborn pup, its muzzle has already stretched out to a most un-Puggish point.

French Connection

"'Tis Hogarth himself and his honest friend Towser,
Inseparate companions! and therefore you see
Cheek by jowl they are drawn in familiar degree;
Both striking the eye with an equal éclat.
The biped This here, and the Quadruped That."

— Anon, *The Scandalizade* (1750)

Certainly we do not deny that there were Pugs in Holland in the eighteenth century or that there may have been traffic in Pugs between Holland and England. But we do maintain that Pugs were universally fashionable in eighteenth-century Europe — no less in France, Germany, Scandinavia, Russia, Spain, and Italy than in Holland and England. Of these many countries, it is France that can boast the earliest unambiguous record of the Pug in Europe. A perfect little fawn Pug is depicted incidentally in a group portrait in the Wallace Collection in London entitled *Louis XIV and His Heirs*, probably executed by a student of Nicolas de Largillière in 1713 or 1714.

The luckiest heir in the painting — Louis XIV's great-grandson, Louis XV — commissioned the second extant record of the Pug in Europe, according to Ellen Brown (1997). In 1730, Jean-Baptiste Oudry — another of Largillière's students, who won appointment as Louis XV's court painter of animals and hunting scenes — painted the portrait of a Pug entitled *Un Carlin* that today graces Le Palais des Beaux-Arts in Lille, France. (In the year that *Un Carlin* was painted, Carlo Bertinazzi was only twenty. Had he really already gained such fame in Paris in the role of Harlequin that dog breeds were being named in his honor?)

Although Brejon de Lavergnée — Head Curator of the Lille — does not share Brown's confidence that the Pug figured in Oudry's picture in fact belonged to his royal patron, a strong royal French connection with the Pug definitely persisted. Louis XV's official mistress after 1744 — the Marquise de Pompadour — kept Pugs. So did her dear friend, Voltaire. So too her later counterpart — Marie-Antoinette. Come 1790, some Pugs paid dearly for that royal connection when the Revolution executed them in the Place de Grève for "a crime that morality prevents us from naming."

From the same year as Oudry's Pug painting come the first records of the European Pug outside France — all in a spate from one man in England. That Pug-besotted individual was the celebrated portraitist and pictorial satirist, Willam Hogarth. Throughout his subsequent career, Hogarth would frequently represent Pugs as a quasi-human actors in the complex social situations parodied in his series of cheap and popular prints. Hogarth may be said to have "broken" the aristocratic Pug to Europe's emerging bourgeois market.

In 1730, Hogarth painted Pugs as social actors in the foregrounds of three of his group portraits of English aristocrats at play. In *The House of Cards* (National Museum of Wales), Hogarth shows a black Pug holding a stick that threatens the teetering house of cards being built by its young mistress. In *The Fountaine Family* (Philadelphia Museum of Art), Hogarth shows a fawn Pug being reprimanded by Lady Fountaine for making off with her picnic basket. In *The Wollaston Family*, Hogarth shows a fawn Pug standing on its hind legs in imitation of the commanding stance of the host of the family gathering.

The model for these three painted Pugs may have been the Pug that Hogarth himself owned at the time — as we know from the first written mention of the Pug in Europe. In an advertisement in the December 5, 1730 issue of the London periodical, *The Craftsman*, Hogarth offered a half-guinea's reward for the return of his lost dog named "Pugg."

After the loss of Pugg, Hogarth owned a series of Pugs that played so salient a part in his public life and art that the artist acquired the sobriquet of "Painter Pugg." Hogarth frequently incorporated Pugs in his paintings and prints as signature devices to satirize the foibles and pretensions of the human figures. In 1735, Hogarth included a pair of Pugs in the fifth plate of *A Rake's Progress*, entitled "Married to an Old Maid": in imitation of Tom Rakewell's cynical exchange of vows with a rich old crone with a glass eye, a trim young Pug addresses his devotions to an ugly old Pug bitch with a glass eye. In 1738, Hogarth's most beloved and most motley Pug — Trump — made his pictorial début in *The Strode Family*: Trump sits dejectedly in an opulent drawing-room while Captain Strode imperiously points down at him with a heavy cane as though castigating his plebian origins.

In 1740, Louis-François Roubiliac — the most important sculptor working in eighteenth-century England — modeled complementary terracotta sculptures of Hogarth and Trump — *Bust of William Hogarth* (National Portrait Gallery) and *Pug* (Victoria and Albert Museum), both of which were later reproduced

in porcelain by the Chelsea pottery factory. In 1745, Hogarth painted Roubiliac's two sculptural subjects face to face in his ironic self-portrait, *The Painter and His Pug* (Tate Gallery), in which Trump patently figures as Hogarth's alter ego.

In another painting of 1745 — *Lord George Graham in his Cabin*, Trump clearly stands in for Hogarth. The subject of this painting was Hogarth's boon companion and fellow senior Mason. Captain Graham in his tasseled slouch-cap settles down in his cabin to enjoy with the ship's purser a bowl of punch, a fowl, a pipe of tobacco, and a private concert by three musicians, one of whom is a dog. Trump is sitting up on his haunches on a chair with a sheet of music propped in front of him like an easel. He is wearing the captain's formal wig, looking for all the world like Handel in his glory.

In his savage satirical print, *The Burlesquer Burlesqued* — subtitled *The Progress of the pug dog in the Art of Painting* — (1753), Paul Sandby unites Hogarth and Trump into a half-man/half-Pug creature who daubs obscenities at an easel while he is brought a bone by a Pug identified by caption as "Jewel." This name had Masonic connotations. Hogarth, having been a London lodge member since 1725, was selected as one of the twelve Stewards of the Grand Lodge of the London Freemasons in 1734. In that capacity, Hogarth designed a "grand Jewel" that would continue to be used in the secret ceremonies of the Stewards well into the nineteenth century. Interestingly, only a few years after Hogarth's elevation, a new German Grand Lodge adopted the Pug as their Masonic emblem.

The Chelsea porcelain versions of Roubiliac's sculpture of Hogarth's Pug were strikingly paralleled in the work of the prolific German sculptor Johann Joachim Kändler, who had been appointed Modellmeister of the Meissen porcelain factory in 1731. The director of the Meissen factory was Count von Brühl, who in 1746 would become the prime minister of Frederick Augustus II, Elector of Saxony. The Elector, who had converted to Roman Catholicism in 1712, also embraced Freemasonry and rose to Grand Master. In 1738, Pope Clement XII promulgated his bull condemning Freemasonry and threatening Catholic Freemasons with excommunication. The Elector thereupon took his lodge underground, reconstituted as the secret *Freimaurerloge vom Mopsorden* (Freemasons' Lodge of the Order of the Pug). Von Brühl curried favor with

the Elector by commissioning Modellmeister Kändler to execute a whole series of exquisite porcelain Pug figures that might serve as secret emblems for the powerful members of the Mopsorden. It is tempting to speculate that the selection in Saxony in the 1740's of the Pug as an artistic subject for Kändler and as a sly emblem for the Elector's lodge was directly inspired by the artistic example of the famous brother Mason who had fashioned the Jewel of their founding lodge in London.

Counting Hogarth's four Pug references in 1730 as one, the fourth record of the Pug in Europe is the entry in Nathan Bailey's *Dictionarium Britannicum* of 1731: "pug, *a Nickname for a Monkey, or Dog.*" Actually, the word *pug* with reference to "monkey" alone is of considerably older vintage, being first attested in 1664. In fashionable drawing-rooms of European capitals in the seventeenth century, marmosets were the pets of choice — highly prized for their dainty little bodies covered with long soft fur; their child-like flattened black faces; and their gentle dispositions that made them amenable to being caressed and dressed like tiny Moorish pages. *Pug* — a popular term of doting address reserved for lovers and children — made a very suitable name for the pampered marmoset.

As an arboreal New World monkey, however, the marmoset admitted of one shocking defect as *mignonette* of the silk-brocaded salon. Back in its South American tree-top habitat, the marmoset is under no adaptive necessity to regulate its excretory functions. It may discharge at will: for all waste products accelerate harmlessly away into the aerial void, neither fouling the home roost nor leaving any trail that predators might follow. Laxity is such a deep-seated instinct in the species that no amount of coaxing or spanking could ever induce the simian Pug to become housebroken. As applied to pet monkeys, a secondary sense of *Pug* — "small demon" — all too often vied with its primary sense as an endearment.

Enter the exotic Lo-sze upon the stage of European high society at the end of the seventeenth century as challenger to the entrenched but enstenched marmoset. The resemblances between FAD lap dogs and marmosets were striking enough to have merited

their own Chinese fable, according to which the original *happa* was the love child of the Lion and the Marmoset. Just like the simian Pug, the canine newcomer boasted a dainty little body; a child-like flattened black face; and a sociable disposition. Nothing could have been more natural than to extend the name for the monkey to its look-alike dog. The canine Pug borrowed its name from the pre-existing simian Pug of the seventeenth century because of its obvious similarities in appearance and social function.

But there was also a telling dissimilarity between the simian and canine Pugs. The little Chinese dog was — by virtue of being a dog — a direct descendant of the wolf: a cursorial predator that closely regulates its excretions in order to mark its hunting ground, advertise its sexual receptivity, and keep its den clean. Consequently, the canine Pug was readily housebroken. Furthermore, the Chinese breeders of the happa dog had long selected for inoffensiveness to the keen olfactory sensitivities of the Chinese court, so that the canine Pug was virtually free of "doggy odor." Finally, the canine Pug's coat

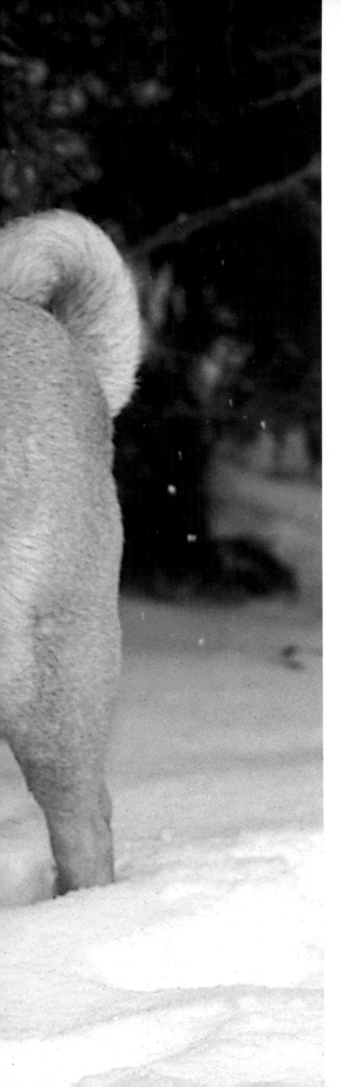

was hygienically short — unlike the marmoset's long fur that was so susceptible to clotting by food and worse. With all of its glowing sanitary advantages, the canine Pug took just a few decades to rout the simian Pug so completely from the drawing-rooms of Europe that the dog snatched from the shocked monkey the very name of *Pug*.

A similar pattern of Pug-dog name derivation from simian antecedents seems to have operated in other Germanic languages as well. As noted above, the German word for Pug is *Mops*, the Dutch cognates of which are *mop*, *mops*, or *mopshond*. Dutch *moppen* means "to pout or grimace, especially like a monkey." In the sixteenth century, the Dutch word was imported into English as part of the expression *mops and mows*, as used in an OED citation from 1581: *The Ape giueth himself to make vs laugh with his mops and mows*. The linguistic evidence joins with the artistic evidence in supporting the conclusions that the Pug dog first appeared in Europe at the end of the seventeenth century; and that within a few decades the Pug dog had driven the Pug monkey out of fashion.

Exactly when and by whose agency the first Pugs arrived in Europe from China is not known. Given, however, that the breeding and ownership of Lo-Sze dogs were legally confined to the Imperial City as exclusive imperial prerogatives, it is plausible to assume that whoever brought the Pug to Europe must have enjoyed such extraordinary favor with the Emperor of China that they were allowed access to the Imperial City and its forbidden fruits.

The Imperial City was truly forbidden. Even a high mandarin or tributary prince could enter this one-and-half mile square walled compound only if commanded to present himself (kow-towing upon his belly) for formal audience. Dutch and English traders were strictly confined to the distant southern delta city of Canton until the First Opium War. Certainly, no Western barbarian of any stripe could ever dream of being granted admission to the Imperial City — unless, that is, he happened to be a Jesuit missionary during the reign of the K'ang-hsi emperor.

K'ang-hsi — second emperor of the Manchu Dynasty, reigning from 1661 to 1722 — has been aptly dubbed the Scholar-Emperor. A prodigious reader himself, K'ang-hsi marshaled an army of Chinese literati to systematize traditional Chinese learning into compendious encyclopedias and

dictionaries. No less ambitious for modern China to close the gap with Europe in science and mathematics, K'ang-hsi relied heavily on the expertise and loyalty of Jesuit scholar-missionaries to this end. In 1666, K'ang-hsi appointed the Flemish Jesuit Ferdinand Verbiest to direct the Imperial Board of Astronomy. As a full member of the mandarin bureacracy in Peking, Vorbiest performed many civil services that endeared him to the Scholar-Emperor: reforming the Chinese calendar; mapping the Empire; translating European scientific treatises into Chinese; casting European cannon for the Chinese army; composing the first Manchu grammar; interpreting between the Chinese and Russians during their treaty negotiations; and tutoring the Emperor himself in Euclid's *Elements*.

To continue Vorbiest's work after his death in 1688, K'ang-hsi enrolled into his court bureacracy many Jesuit scholar-missionaries — notably the Frenchmen Jean-François Gerbillon, Pierre Jartoux, Jean-Baptiste Régis, and Joachim Bouvet. So pleased was K'ang-Hsi with their performance that he promulgated a law in 1692 authorizing the Jesuits to

proselytize anywhere in the Empire. When the Jesuits cured K'ang-hsi of malaria several years later, he rewarded them with the ultimate mark of his favor. The emperor mandated the permanent establishment within the very walls of his Imperial City of a Roman Catholic church and residence for the French fathers. This Jesuit mission — called Pei-tang ("North Church") — he caused to be built just a stone's throw over the Pei-hai ("North Sea") from the White Dagoba that his father had built for the Dalai Lama. (Two centuries later, the sanctuary at Pei-tang would be the site of the Boxers' massacre of four hundred Chinese Christians by order of the Empress Dowager.)

Here opens a clear window of opportunity for the transmission of the *Lo-sze ba-erh* from China to Europe. The Jesuit mandarinate of Peking had been elevated to a status co-equal with the Office of Household, by which they were given the freedom of the Imperial City and the domestic perquisites of functionaries in daily attendance on the Emperor. Among the perquisites of residential courtiers, as we have noted, was the privilege of owning *Lo-szes*. Yet the

Jesuits of the Imperial City were not merely courtiers. Pre-eminently, they were legates of the Roman Church and cultural ambassadors of their royal patrons back in Europe. As such, Peking Jesuits periodically shuttled back and forth to Europe.

Now, a Jesuit scholar stationed in the Imperial City who had become attached to his *Lo-szes* would not part willingly with his charming little companions if he were obliged to return to Europe. Since his privileged status exempted him from the usual interdiction against removing *Lo-szes* from the Imperial City, a repatriated Jesuit would not scruple to pack his *Lo-szes* along with his scrolls and instruments for the long voyage home to Europe.

Back in Europe, a Jesuit bearing credentials as scholar and diplomatist to the Emperor of China would be received with intense interest at the court of his royal patron. If the bicultural Jesuit were to exhibit his *Lo-szes* to the court along with his mandarin dress and maps, the exotic appearance and courtly manners of the little protegés would surely pique royal curiosity. In an age in which a token of royal amusement was tantamount to a command, assimilation of *Lo-szes* into the royal family entourage would naturally follow.

The history of one of the French Jesuits of the Imperial City strikingly illustrates the plausibility of our scenario. In 1688 — the year of Vorbiest's death — there arrived in Peking a French Jesuit mathematician named Joachim Bouvet whom Louis XIV himself had selected and underwritten for the Jesuit mission to China. Well-pleased with this erudite member of the *Académie des Sciences* whom the King of France had hand-picked for him, Emperor K'ang-hsi attached Father Bouvet as his personal tutor in mathematics to succeed the late Father Vorbeist. Like Vorbeist, Bouvet was an able linguist. Besides composing a Chinese dictionary, Bouvet wrote mathematical treatises in the Tartar language for which the Emperor himself wrote the prefaces. Having donated the Jesuits their own residence in the Imperial City, K'ang-hsi desired to fill it with more French academicians of Bouvet's caliber.

In 1697, accordingly, K'ang-hsi sent Bouvet back to Paris to fetch more missionaries. Bouvet presented to Louis XIV a gift from the Emperor (forty-nine precious Chinese volumes) along with the Emperor's request for more missionaries. Between court appearances in 1697, Father Bouvet busied

himself with the publication of two books that he had written on China. Louis entrusted Bouvet with ten missionaries and an opulently bound collection of engravings for the Emperor of China, to whom Bouvet returned in 1699.

One of the two books that Bouvet published in Paris in 1697 — *Portrait historique de l'Empereur de la Chine* — came into such hot demand in Europe's China-mad court circles that it was soon translated into Latin and republished for the international market. Bouvet's translator was the salaried genealogist of the Duke of Brunswick-Lüneburg. His job of validating the House of Brunswick's claims to the electorate of Hanover and later to the throne of England was a big one but not so onerous as to preclude work on a boggling assortment of extracurricular interests. He wrote political pamphlets against the expansionist policies of Louis XIV. He wrote pamphlets for the peaceful reunion of the Catholic and Protestant churches. He carried on an extensive correspondence with Father Bouvet on the application of his new binary number system to the elucidation of the *I Ching*.

Never one to veg out after a tough day in the library validating his employer's pedigree, he also employed his spare time to write up a nifty mathematical method of his own invention — known today as *the calculus*. And Gottfried Leibniz was his name-o.

The reader gently reminds us, however, that the present work is not entitled *For the Love of Calculus*. The identity of Bouvet's translator is less germane to our present argument about the origin of the Pug in Europe than is the identity of the person to whom Bouvet dedicated his book. Bouvet dedicated his book about his East Coast boss, the Son of Heaven, to his West Coast boss, the Sun King.

Now recall what we have already proved to be the first genuine evidence of the Pug in Europe, from *c.* 1713: namely, the Pug depicted in the family portrait of *Louis XIV and His Heirs*. Aha! Our hypothesis that the Pug first came to Europe via the French Jesuit Connection at the end of the seventeenth century — whether as an official gift of the Emperor of China or as a Jesuit missionary's show-and-tell sidekick — is seen to commit no violence against historical

plausibility. It is entirely plausible that Bouvet (or one of his French Jesuit colleagues in the Imperial City) might have introduced the Pug to the court of Louis XIV. (In this connection, it is entirely implausible that the same monarch who had revoked the Edict of Nantes would permit some Dog Who Had Saved Protestantism to besmirch his official dynastic portrait.)

Once established in the trend-setting court of Louis XIV, the Pug fashion might be expected to have been aped by the less magnificent courts of neighboring principalities — such as the electorates of Hanover and Saxony. Would it not be ironic if descendants of Bouvet's little dogs were chosen to accompany the Elector of Hanover to England to be crowned King George I in 1714; while Bouvet's promethean correspondent — disappointed in his own hopes of being invited along to London — had to stay behind to grind out the Brunswick annals?

It is also intriguing to speculate why the Elector of Saxony should have adopted the Pug as the emblem of his Freemason lodge after the papal bull of 1737 had driven it underground. On the one hand, the Pug was an appropriate emblem for a lodge headed by a Catholic prince insofar as the Pug was a "good Catholic" dog, having been acquired by a pious Catholic monarch from the hands of his Jesuit emissaries. On the other hand, the Pug was an appropriate emblem for a lodge whose rank-and-file membership was the Lutheran nobility of Saxony. Through the Pug metaphor, the Saxon Freemasons appealed to the Pope for restoration of only as much tolerance as the Jesuits had formerly shown the pagan emperor K'ang-hsi and the Protestant philosopher Leibniz.

We have shown that the Pug was definitely not the Dog Who Saved Protestantism in the sixteenth century. We have shown that the preponderance of evidence instead suggests that during the early eighteenth century the Pug evolved in religious affiliation from Buddhist to Catholic to Deist.

One Swallow

"One swallow does not a summer make — any more than one painting, sculpture or carving can prove the origin of a breed."

— Hilary Harmar,
The Complete Chihuahua Encyclopaedia (1972)

Just as a disorderly marmoset pug could shock the decorum of an eighteenth-century salon, so an out-of-order Pug dog could wreck the argument of the last two chapters. Much ink was spilled in the preceding chapters to lend color to the hypothesis that the first Pugs did not appear in Europe until late in the reign of Louis XIV, having been brought from the Imperial City to the French court by Jesuit missionaries. The plausibility of this hypothesis hinges on the validity of the premise that the "perfect little fawn Pug" painted with *Louis XIV and His Heirs* in *c.* 1713 constitutes "the earliest unambiguous record of the Pug in Europe."

What if this underlying assertion were untrue? What if an unambiguous record of the Pug in Europe could be produced from an earlier period? Then the whole case for the priority of the French and for the agency of the Jesuits in the transmission of the Chinese Pug to Europe would collapse like a children's house of cards trampled by a frisky Pug.

Several putative records of the Pug in Europe prior to 1713 have already been examined and found wanting. The most commonly alleged prior record — that of the Prince of Orange's "Camus" in 1572 — was shown to refer to a completely different breed. Less commonly alleged earlier records — the English portraits by Kneller (1698) and Knyff (*c.* 1702) — were shown to be ambiguous as well as only marginally earlier.

Long predating all these alleged earlier records, however, is one that has not — to the best of our knowledge — been hitherto advanced as possibly representing a Pug. The record in question hails back a full three centuries earlier. Between 1415 and 1422, young Pisanello (1395–1455/6) compiled a studio album of pen-and-ink sketches from life, now preserved in the Louvre as the *Codex Vallardi*. These drawings — many of them executed with startlingly modern naturalistic facility — include dog studies. Pisanello's justly famous drawing of a Greyhound renders every familiar feature of that ancient breed with delicate clarity.

Much less well known is Pisanello's study of another dog in the form of six deft little character sketches. This sejant dog is represented from a variety of angles and wearing a variety of tragicomic expressions that range from high dudgeon to lugubrious incredulity to groveling ingratiation. Pisanello can impart such a diversity of vivid anthropomorphic expression to this dog's face because it is so amenably human-like in its physical configuration. The dog's face is arrestingly flat; his eyes are prominent and contained in the flat plane of the face; his nose is small and pert; his mouth is bowed in a defiant pout; his ears are triangular pendant flaps. In short, Pisanello has drawn us a dog with the achondroplastic head of a Pug.

Although the head of Pisanello's dog is essentially that of a modern Pug, his body is not. The limbs, trunk, and tail of Pisanello's dog are proportionately much longer than those of the modern Pug. Although the parts of the dog do not seem to be knit in the neat proportions that characterize some midgets, the absence of scale in Pisanello's drawings leaves the dog's overall body-size an open question. Unlike the modern Pug, Pisanello's

dog is definitely free of micromelic achondroplasia (and possibly also of pituitary dwarfism). Is Pisanello's dog on that account not a Pug?

Not necessarily. Recall that micromelic achondroplasia was not superimposed on the Pug's facial achondroplasia and pituitary dwarfism as a defining characteristic of the European breed until the third quarter of the nineteenth century, when English Pug-breeders embraced the post-1860 wave of micromelic *Lo-sze baerh* imports from China. All prior images of the European Pug — from the early eighteenth through the middle of the nineteenth centuries — depict an animal with relatively long and slender legs.

The stunting of the breed's extremities came even later to America. As late as 1898, long-legged Pugs were taking prizes at Westminster. A 1894 studio photograph of the dame of these Westminster winners, Haughty Madge, shows an animal so uncannily like Pisanello's dog in form and feature that one might almost credit that it was she who posed for that International Gothic artist.

By themselves, then, the long legs of Pisanello's

dog do not disqualify him from being labeled an historical "Pug." On the strength of his Pug-like face alone, therefore, Pisanello's dog would seem to refute irresistibly the argument of the last two chapters that the history of the European Pug did not begin until the turn of the seventeenth century. Or does he?

To assess the significance of Pisanello's dog to the history of the Pug breed, a serious problem of contextual continuity must be recognized. Within two decades of the painting of *Louis XIV and his heirs* in c. 1713, Pug-images spread across European art in a torrent that has never since abated. In stark contrast to this uninterrupted tradition of the Pug in art over the last three centuries, the three centuries that separate Pisanello's dog from Louis XIV's are absolutely devoid of Pug images.

If the Pug were a species and paintings were fossils, a paleontologist would conclude as a matter of course that the three-century hiatus in Pug fossils after 1415 was just an accident. Conditions conducive to the formation and preservation of Pug-fossils simply had not obtained. The Pug species itself must

assuredly have remained in continuous existence during the fossil hiatus, for it is impossible in nature for a species to appear, go extinct, and then re-appear.

But the Pug is not a species. The Pug is a breed. Human beings have developed their hundreds of dog breeds by selecting particular bundles of traits from the protean gamut of genetic potentialities inherent in the 78 chromosomes of the species *Canis familiaris*. Unlike natural species, artificial breeds can indeed appear, go extinct, and then re-appear. Any dog breed that has undergone extinction or adulteration can be quite routinely re-created or purified by a competent breeder to exact specifications.

Examples abound of extinct breeds that have been deliberately re-created in accordance with antique art-images. In most actual cases, the motive for rehabilitating an ancient dog breed has been to animate a nationalistic myth. Such are the Cavalier King Charles Spaniel (developed in the 1920s in imitation of the toy spaniels in English royal portraits of the seventeenth century); the Great Dane (developed in nineteenth-century Germany in imitation of the hulking Alaunts that adorn hunts and battles in medieval German art; declared the state dog of Bismarck's Germany); the Canaan Dog (developed in the 1930s by a German Jewish kibbutznik in imitation of a dog depicted in four-thousand-year-old Palestinian cave-drawings); and even our little friend, the Kooikerhondje (developed in the 1940s during the German occupation by a Dutch patriot in imitation of the Kooiker's omnipresent image in seventeenth-century Dutch painting).

We certainly do not mean to suggest by analogy that the eighteenth-century European Pug was a deliberate re-creation of Pisanello's fifteenth-century dog. Rather, we mean only to establish the principle that successive representations in 1415 and 1713 of two dogs that appear to be of the same breed cannot be taken necessarily to imply genetic descent from the former to the latter.

More strongly, we would urge that the absence of any image of the Pug in European art between 1415 and 1713 argues forcefully against continuous descent. Portraiture from this long interval copiously documents the continuous presence of such lap dogs as the toy spaniel and the Maltese. Unquestionably, no lap dog breed could have survived across this three-hundred-year interval without noble patronage. The

odds that the Pug could have enjoyed noble patronage all that while — yet not once have edged out the competition to grace some lady's portrait — are vanishingly small.

(One dubious exception may be entertained against the statement that no Pug-like images survive from the period from 1415 to 1713. A bizarre early painting by Jacopo da Empoli dating to 1575 represents a hideously bloated man in knickers surrounded by twelve shortfaced lap dogs in a formal garden. Most of these dogs are clearly classifiable as toy spaniels or Maltese. A few, however, are short-haired and might be said to resemble Pugs in that respect. Their patchy coat coloring, however, is that of the spaniels. The painting is oddly compelling but technically crude. As a result, the breed identity of the shorthaired dogs is highly ambiguous.)

All things considered, Pisanello's dog cuts such a solipsistically singular and temporally isolated figure in the historical record that he cannot be brought to constrain the discourse of the last two chapters. The historical *mise-en-scène* for Pisanello's dog is a black box. No speculation concern-

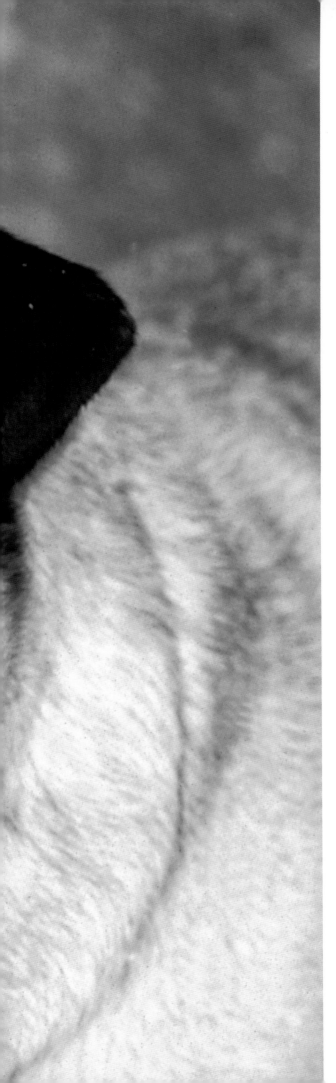

ing lineage and provenance can be ruled out as contrary to the preponderance of evidence when we have no evidence at all.

Apart from taste, there are no grounds for preferring one line of speculation to another. Perhaps Pisanello's dog was a freak mongrel carrying an errant mutant gene for facial achondroplasia. Perhaps he was a specimen of a locally developed breed homologous to the future Pug that failed to win wider acceptance and went extinct without further trace. Perhaps he was an imported one-off curiosity smuggled from China to Venice, where Pisanello was working at the time. Or perhaps he embodies the authentic Ur-Pug — originating in Europe and exported to China (for he is after all three centuries older than the first image we have of a Chinese Pug)!

Pisanello's dog is not the only instance of an early art-image of a dog whose apparent breed identity seems perversely out of joint with the rest of that breed's attested history. One of the sons of Jethro in Sandro Botticelli's fresco, *Scenes from the Life of Moses*, painted in the Sistine Chapel in 1481/2, carries under his arm a tiny, prick-eared, bug-eyed, long-nailed, short-haired dog that looks the spitting image of a modern Chihuahua. A dog of identical description is figured in Vittore Carpaccio's *Two Courtesans* (Correr Museum, Venice), painted sometime between 1495 and 1500.

What is incongruous about these Quattrocento images of this Chihuahuaoid is that no importations of the Chihuahua from Mexico to Europe are recorded until the 1870s. Except for these two nearly coeval Italian paintings from the late fifteenth century, not one conceivable allusion to the presence of the Chihuahua in Europe is to be found anywhere in European art or literature prior to the late nineteenth century.

Throughout Mexico, by contrast, ceramic effigies of Chihuahua-like dogs (though not, on account of their stylization, so unequivocally Chihuahua-like as Botticelli's dog) have been recovered from a continuum of pre-Columbian sites going all the way back to first-century Teotihuacan. Descriptions of Chihuahua-like dogs recur in the literature of colonial Mexico, beginning with the detailed accounts of the Franciscan missionary Fray Bernadino de Sahagún in the early sixteenth century.

It seems safe to assert, therefore, that the Mexican Chihuahuaoid predates Botticelli's Chihuahuaoid. Is it safe to conclude that the latter therefore was genetically descended

from the former? Not likely! Who would be so daring as to interpret Botticelli's dog of 1481 as proof that commercial intercourse between Europe and Mexico flourished a decade before Columbus sailed the ocean blue?

Like Pisanello's dog, Botticelli's dog is wrapped in mystery. The phantasmagoria of speculative possibilities that was conjured up to account for the presence of Pisanello's Pugoid in Venice also dances around Botticelli's Chihuahuaoid in Rome. Was he a freak individual? A product of convergent development of independent breeds on opposite sides of the Atlantic Ocean? A one-off import item from Mexico via the hypothetical Chinese merchant trade? A specimen of some erstwhile native Chinese, European, or African breed that was exported to Mexico prior to its home extinction? None of these lines of speculation is either contradicted or corroborated by any independent historical facts. Unless some supplementary records are uncovered, Botticelli's Chihuahuaoid must remain a cipher that cannot be assigned a meaningful place in the history of the modern Chihuahua breed.

Just so for the place of Pisanello's dog in the history of the modern Pug breed. Barring new discoveries of unambiguous Pug-images from the period 1481–1713, Pisanello's dog is simply too remote and disconnected from the continuous post-1713 narrative history of the Pug breed to undermine the argument of the last two chapters.

Still, we are not entirely untroubled by the malaise of *déjà vu* as we return the *Codex Vallardi* to its drawer in the Louvre at closing time. When we arrive back home and are greeted at the door by a joyous onrush of Pug, the *Codex* images seem to flash into life before our eyes. The specular eyes of Pisanello's dog seem to fix ours across six centuries like those of an overwrought little sphinx bursting with a mute riddle: "Try this on for size, smarty-pants: 'What is has a flat face, normal-sized body, and four normal-length legs in the morning? A flat face, midget body, and four normal-length legs at noon? And a flat face, midget body, and four dwarf legs in the evening?' Come on, come on, you big dummy... the suspense is killing me!"

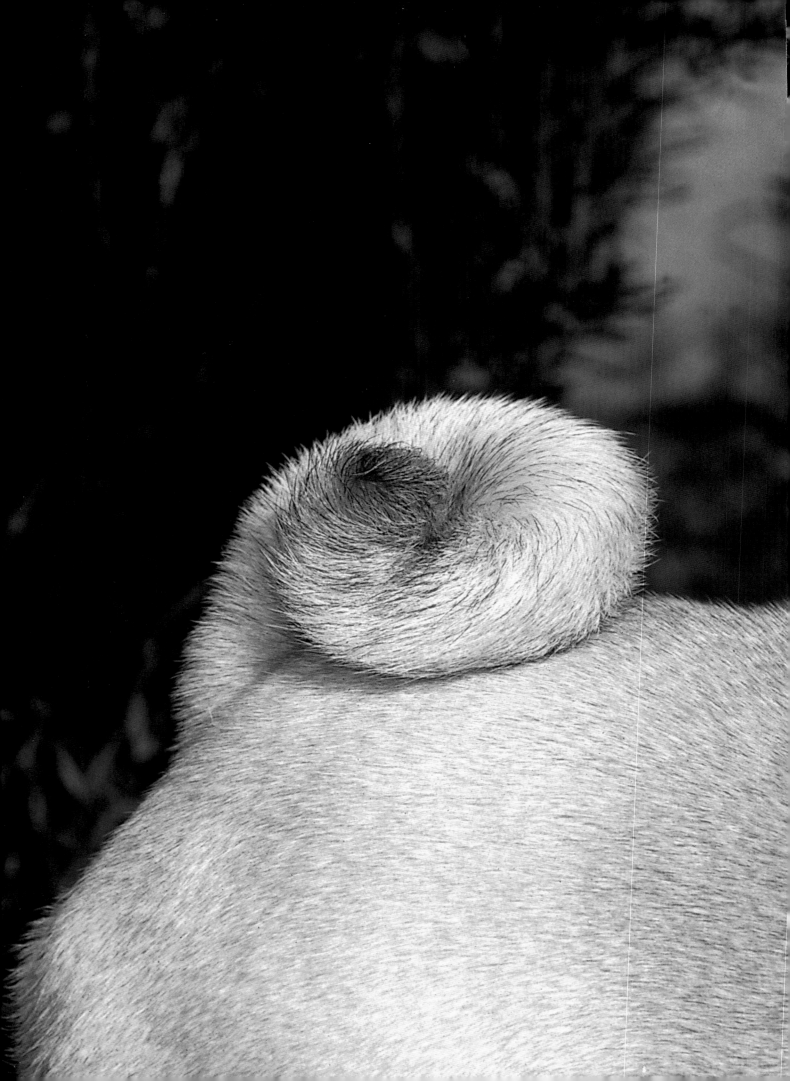